T0312302

Cambridge Elements ≡

Elements in the Philosophy of Physics
edited by
James Owen Weatherall
University of California, Irvine

PHILOSOPHY OF PARTICLE PHYSICS

Porter Williams
University of Pittsburgh

CAMBRIDGE
UNIVERSITY PRESS

Shaftesbury Road, Cambridge CB2 8EA, United Kingdom

One Liberty Plaza, 20th Floor, New York, NY 10006, USA

477 Williamstown Road, Port Melbourne, VIC 3207, Australia

314–321, 3rd Floor, Plot 3, Splendor Forum, Jasola District Centre, New Delhi – 110025, India

103 Penang Road, #05–06/07, Visioncrest Commercial, Singapore 238467

Cambridge University Press is part of Cambridge University Press & Assessment, a department of the University of Cambridge.

We share the University's mission to contribute to society through the pursuit of education, learning and research at the highest international levels of excellence.

www.cambridge.org
Information on this title: www.cambridge.org/9781009205399

DOI: 10.1017/9781009205382

First published 2023

A catalogue record for this publication is available from the British Library.

ISBN 978-1-009-20539-9 Paperback
ISSN 2632-413X (online)
ISSN 2632-4121 (print)

Philosophy of Particle Physics

Elements in the Philosophy of Physics

DOI: 10.1017/9781009205382
First published online: July 2023

Porter Williams
University of Pittsburgh

Author for correspondence: Porter Williams, pdw27@pitt.edu

Abstract: This Element offers an introduction to selected philosophical issues that arise in contemporary particle physics, aimed at philosophers who have limited prior exposure to quantum field theory. On the one hand, it critically surveys philosophical work on the representation of particles in quantum field theory, the formal machinery and conceptual implications of renormalization and renormalization group methods, and ontological and methodological questions raised by the use of effective field theory techniques in particle physics. On the other hand, it identifies topics in particle physics that have not yet received philosophical attention and sketches avenues for philosophical analysis of those topics. The primary aim of the Element is to provide philosophers of physics with an entry point into the literature on the philosophy of particle physics and identify interesting directions for future research for students and researchers alike.

Keywords: quantum field theory, particle physics, scientific realism, renormalization, effective field theory

ISBNs: 9781009205399 (PB), 9781009205382 (OC)
ISSNs: 2632-413X (online), 2632-4121 (print)

Contents

1 Introduction

Elementary particle physics is the study of the fundamental building blocks of nature: the quarks and leptons that make up all (nondark) matter; the gauge bosons that carry the electromagnetic, weak, and strong forces; and the Higgs boson that generates the masses of these elementary particles via the Higgs mechanism. Although they are the building blocks of the everyday objects around us, we can only study the properties of many of these particles by creating extreme conditions quite unlike those in everyday life. While one can gain valuable insight into the behavior of elementary particles from cosmology and astrophysics, the most successful way to create such conditions has been through high-energy collisions in particle accelerators like the Large Hadron Collider (LHC) at CERN.

The mathematical framework used to model elementary particles and their behavior is quantum field theory (QFT). This framework incorporates the principles of quantum mechanics and special relativity, both of which are indispensable for describing the extreme conditions we create to study elementary particles. Quantum field theory is an expansive and rich theoretical edifice that is the workhorse of modern physics; it has valuable applications in many areas outside of particle physics, particularly cosmology and condensed matter physics. (The history of its development, which extends from the 1920s through the present day, is fascinating and often helpful for understanding its modern structure; for entry points, see Schweber (1994), Kaiser (2009), and Duncan (2012, chapters 1–2).) The successful "theories" in elementary particle physics most likely to be familiar to nonphysicists – quantum electrodynamics (QED), quantum chromodynamics (QCD), the Standard Model of particle physics itself – are each particular models of the general framework of QFT.

Yet it is an unfinished framework. The mathematical architecture of QFT is not yet completely understood, to say nothing of the lack of consensus about its conceptual foundations. The result is that there are a handful of distinct but related mathematical frameworks, all of which have some claim to the name "quantum field theory." (See Swanson (2017) for a discussion of how to exploit the variety of frameworks for QFT to investigate its conceptual implications.) Many of these frameworks were developed with the goal of placing QFT on a mathematically secure footing, a challenge first tackled in earnest in the 1950s and remarkably resistant to resolution. Much philosophical analysis of QFT has taken place within one or another of these mathematically rigorous frameworks. The virtue of these frameworks is that they often allow for mathematically precise formulations of conceptually interesting questions that sometimes even admit mathematically rigorous resolution, promising a readily available precision and conceptual clarity to which many philosophers are attracted. A number of advances have been made in such work, and for more extensive discussion I encourage the reader to explore Swanson (forthcoming) as a companion to this Element.

The vice of these frameworks is that, at least presently, they lack the tools required to apply QFT to the actual world. To find models of QFT that can be applied in particle physics and elsewhere, one must turn to the framework for QFT found in most quantum field theory textbooks, taught in university physics departments, and employed by workaday physicists in their research. The mathematical foundations of this framework are shaky, but its predictive successes are unprecedented. In recent years, philosophers have begun to complement the earlier work on foundational questions in QFT conducted in mathematically rigorous frameworks with philosophical investigations carried out using the QFT more familiar to practicing physicists. This framework for QFT offers novel avenues of approach to questions familiar from earlier philosophical investigation of QFT and raises new, foundationally pressing questions of its own. As one might expect in a volume devoted to foundational aspects of particle physics, I will work within this framework for QFT.

My focus on QFT as it is employed in particle physics has two consequences. The first consequence stems from the essentially tautological statement that particle physics is done by particle physicists. They are human actors with particular scientific goals and familiar human cognitive limitations, and these combine to produce epistemological challenges. In particular, challenges associated with the search for new physics receive attention at several points, particularly theoretical heuristics that shape expectations about where to direct experimental searches for new physics. (For an entry point into the large literature on epistemological challenges presented by experimental physics more generally, see Boyd (2021).) The second consequence is that the models of QFT applied in particle physics provide accurate descriptions of nature over a restricted set of length scales, but offer physically misleading or mathematically inconsistent descriptions of nature when pushed beyond those scales. Models like this are called *effective field theories* (EFT), and this Element is organized around providing an introduction to the mathematical structure, characteristic patterns of inference, and conceptual implications of EFT.

The Element is structured as follows. In Section 2, I provide a selective introduction to the structure of QFT. A central activity in particle physics is the calculation of probability distributions for the outcomes of scattering experiments, information that is encoded in the *S-matrix*. After introducing necessary preliminaries about QFT, discussion in Section 2 focuses on the essentials of scattering theory. In Section 3, I turn to a complex issue: the concept of "particle" in QFT. I focus on two aspects: (1) the connection between symmetries of a spacetime and possible properties of particles in that spacetime, famously identified by Wigner in 1939, and (2) the inability to define states of a quantum field that correspond to a particle strictly localized in any bounded region of spacetime. In Section 4, I focus on renormalization methods. Initially introduced by Schwinger, Tomonaga, Feynman, and Dyson in the immediate wake of World War II, renormalization is a necessary step in most calculations performed in QFT but was initially a source of considerable consternation among physicists. However, spurred by mathematical innovations by Wilson, Fisher, Kadanoff, and others, the understanding of the physical meaning of renormalization methods underwent an important transformation in the 1970s. In Section 5, I present the EFT framework. My primary focus is on the reasoning underlying various uses of EFT methods in particle physics and the unique patterns of inference licensed by the EFT framework. I also critically evaluate two popular heuristics that guide expectations in particle physics about the scale(s) at which new physics will be discovered. I conclude by summarizing philosophical work about whether the successes of EFT methods support a scientific realist attitude toward those successful models.

Throughout the Element, I emphasize basic structural features of QFT and the patterns of reasoning that connect them. I occasionally point out as-yet-unexplored avenues of philosophical inquiry that strike me as promising. Because of its introductory nature and short length, I do not delve into technical niceties and am cavalier about issues like normalization and prefactors when no conceptual matter is at stake. There are many, many good QFT textbooks available in which those details are waiting for the interested reader.

Finally, a word about notation: particle physicists typically use "natural units" in which $\hbar = c = 1$. This lets us write all dimensionful quantities, like length, mass, or time, as powers of energy. To give some perspective on the scales involved in particle physics, the conversion of the SI units for length, mass, and time into natural units are given next. The unit of energy is electronvolts (eV), with $1 \text{ GeV} = 10^9 \text{ eV}$.

$1 \text{ GeV}^{-1} = 1.97327 \times 10^{-16} \text{ meters}$
$1 \text{ GeV}^{-1} = 6.58212 \times 10^{-25} \text{ seconds}$
$1 \text{ GeV} = 1.78266 \times 10^{-24} \text{ grams}$

2 Quantum Field Theory

Quantum field theory is the mathematical framework that describes the quantum mechanical behavior of fields. A field is a map that assigns a mathematical object to every point on a spacetime manifold $\mathcal{M}$. The use of fields to describe physical systems is indispensible in classical and quantum physics, from the classical mechanics of continua to the description of physics on the worldsheet in string theory. Unsurprisingly, the type of mathematical object assigned to each spacetime point depends on the properties of the physical system being described. For example, suppose one wanted to assign a temperature to every point in a spacetime region $\mathcal{O}$ – my office, for example, or the surface of the Pacific Ocean. Temperature can be fully specified by a single real number, its magnitude, and so one would assign to every point in $\mathcal{O}$ a real number. This is an example of a real-valued scalar field, a map that assigns to every point in $\mathcal{O}$ a real number: the value of the temperature at that point. A more complicated physical system, like an electric field, has more physical degrees of freedom than temperature and we require a mathematical description that reflects that. The electric field at a spacetime point has both a magnitude and a direction and so is described by a vector-valued field, a map that assigns a vector to every spacetime point. Yet more complicated systems with more physical degrees of freedom, like the spacetime metric in general relativity, require yet more information to be fully described; in this case, a tensor-valued field that assigns a tensor to every point in spacetime. One could multiply examples ad infinitum; the point is that there are many useful types of field, and the use of any particular field is dictated by the physical properties of the system one aims to describe.

These examples are of field-theoretic descriptions that encode the information necessary for doing classical physics. To describe the quantum behavior of those fields, one requires QFT. A quantum field is a map that assigns an *operator* to every point on a spacetime manifold $\mathcal{M}$. (More precisely, mathematical consistency requires that quantum field operators be "smeared" over infinitesimal regions of spacetime Streater and Wightman (1964, chapter 3).) Like the classical fields mentioned above, mathematical properties of these operators depend on the physical properties of the system being modeled. A quantum analogue of a temperature field, for example, can be described by assigning a quantized scalar field $\varphi(x, t)$ to every point in spacetime. The additional physical degrees of freedom possessed by the electromagnetic field mean that it is described by a quantized vector field $A_\mu(x, t)$, while the physical properties of electrons and positrons are reflected in the fact that they are described by a quantized spinor field $\Psi(x, t)$. What exactly it means to say that an operator-valued field is a "vector field" or a "scalar field" will get cleared up in our discussion of representations of the Poincaré group in Section 3. For now, what matters is that to describe the quantum mechanical behavior of fields, one assigns operators to points in spacetime.

Describing the quantum mechanical behavior of fields requires the mathematical structure of quantum mechanics, of course. Furthermore, although QFT has valuable applications in a number of settings, our interest is in elementary particles in Minkowski spacetime. This means that we will also require the mathematical structure of special relativity. (One can model quantum fields in many other spacetime settings, from Galilean spacetime to de Sitter or anti-de Sitter spacetimes, but we will restrict ourselves to Minkowski spacetime.) I presume that readers have at least some familiarity with both quantum mechanics and special relativity, but a brief reminder of some relevant features provides a useful avenue of approach to QFT.

The mathematical structure of special relativity, for our purposes, is captured by the symmetry group of Minkowski spacetime, the Poincaré group. In the next section we will explore a deep connection between representations of this group and the concept of a particle in QFT, but for now we remind ourselves of some of its basic structure. The Poincaré group consists of the isometries of Minkowski spacetime: transformations that do not change the spacetime interval between two points, as determined by the Minkowski metric $\eta_{\mu\nu}$. In fact, one typically considers a restricted version of the Poincaré group that excludes isometries that change the sign of any of the spacetime coordinates (i.e., parity or time-reversal transformations). This group is called the *restricted* Poincaré group and it consists of orthochronous Lorentz transformations – transformations composed of spatial rotations and Lorentz boosts – and translations in spacetime.

In particle physics, the empirical predictions of models of QFT are required to be invariant under Poincaré transformations. These are quantum theories, so these predictions take the form of probability distributions over the possible outcomes of experimental measurements. As long as these predictions are Poincaré invariant, any two observers whose frames of reference are related by a Poincaré transformation will agree on the probability that any particular event will occur at a given point in spacetime – that a muon will register in a particle detector, for example. Enforcing the requirement of Poincaré invariance at the level of empirical predictions generates a number of deeper constraints on the theoretical structure of QFT. We will encounter one of the most important of these in the next section.

The basic mathematical structure of quantum mechanics appears in QFT much like it appears in the nonrelativistic quantum theories familiar to philosophers. The space of possible states of a quantum field is a Hilbert space $\mathcal{H}$; each physical system is associated with an algebra $\mathcal{A}$ of linear operators acting on $\mathcal{H}$, with observable properties of the field represented by Hermitian elements of that algebra; and the dynamical evolution of the states of the field is determined by a privileged Hermitian operator, the Hamiltonian H. This structural continuity between nonrelativistic quantum theories and QFT is often explained most clearly in mathematically rigorous presentations, such as Haag (1996) or Strocchi (2013), and is rarely foregrounded in textbook presentations of QFT. Nevertheless, it is there. In the brief introduction to QFT in this section, we will emphasize this common mathematical structure.

2.1 States

For now, we will restrict ourselves to the simplest example of a quantum field: the free real scalar field $\varphi(x, t)$. The label "free" means that excitations of this field – its associated particle – do not interact with one another. States of this field can be understood to describe multiple, noninteracting particles. We will introduce some simple machinery to construct the states of this free scalar field: creation and annihilation operators. Our goal is to see how the formalism of creation and annihilation operators can be used to construct the entire Hilbert space of states associated with this free field $\varphi(x, t)$, to see that these creation and annihilation operators provide a useful representation of the quantum field itself, and to use them to clarify the relationship between the field operators $\varphi(x, t)$ and other elements of the algebra $\mathcal{A}$ of operators.

Suppose the field $\varphi(x, t)$ is in its ground state, that is, its lowest-energy state: a state with no particles. This state is called the vacuum and we will label it $|0\rangle$. To construct the additional states in $\mathcal{H}$, we can introduce creation and annihilation operators $a^\dagger$ and a that add or remove a particle from a state and apply them to the vacuum state. A real scalar field has no "internal" degrees of freedom (i.e., no degrees of freedom other than momentum and position), so the creation and annihilation operators can be labeled $a_p^\dagger$ and a_p: they create and annihilate particles with 4-momentum $p^\mu = (E_p, \mathbf{p})$. In general, creation and annihilation operators add or remove particles with properties, or "quantum numbers," determined by the associated quantum field; for example, for a fermionic field these operators would be labeled by momentum and spin. (We label particles by their spatial momenta, with the understanding that they satisfy the relativistic mass–energy relation $E_p^2 = p^2 + m^2$, where m is the rest mass of the particle. In the rest frame of the particle, where 3-momentum $p = 0$, this becomes $E = m$, which is $E = mc^2$ in natural units.)

Beginning with the vacuum state $|0\rangle$, one can construct states of the field describing multiple noninteracting particles as follows:

$$a_p^\dagger |0\rangle = |p\rangle, \quad a_{p'}^\dagger a_p^\dagger |0\rangle = |p, p'\rangle, \quad a_{p''}^\dagger a_{p'}^\dagger a_p^\dagger |0\rangle = |p, p', p''\rangle, \ldots$$

The first is a state of the field containing a single particle with momentum p; the second is a state of the field containing two noninteracting particles, one with momentum p and the other with momentum p'; and so on. Similarly, the action of the annihilation operator is defined as follows:

$$\ldots, a_{p''}\,|p,p',p''\rangle = |p,p'\rangle, \quad a_{p'}a_p\,|p,p'\rangle = |0\rangle, \quad a_p\,|0\rangle = 0.$$

A defining property of the vacuum state $|0\rangle$ is that it is the unique state in $\mathcal{H}$ that returns zero when acted on by *any* annihilation operator a_p.

As one might suspect, *any* multiparticle state of the quantum field $\varphi(x,t)$ can be constructed by appropriate applications of creation operators to the vacuum state:

$$|p_1^{n_1}, p_2^{n_2}, \ldots, p_r^{n_r}\rangle \propto (a_p^\dagger)^{n_1}(a_{p_2}^\dagger)^{n_2}\ldots(a_{p_r}^\dagger)^{n_r}\,|0\rangle,$$

where n_j labels the number of particles with momentum p_j. (This representation of the state is called the *occupation number* representation: n_j labels the number of particles occupying a particular momentum mode p_j.)

Every state of the free real scalar field $\varphi(x,t)$ can be constructed via this procedure: one can construct the entire Hilbert space for a free quantum field by acting on its vacuum state with (linear combinations of) creation and annihilation operators. This Hilbert space consisting of states that describe multiple, noninteracting particles is called a Fock space. It plays a central role in the formulation of scattering theory, a central aspect of QFT that we will describe shortly.

The commutation relations that hold between creation and annihilation operators encode information about the physical system with which they are associated. For bosons, they obey the following commutation relations:

$$[a_{p\sigma}, a_{p'\sigma'}] = 0 = [a_{p\sigma}^\dagger, a_{p'\sigma'}^\dagger], \quad [a_{p\sigma}, a_{p'\sigma'}^\dagger] = \delta(p-p')\delta_{\sigma\sigma'},$$

where the index σ stands for any additional quantum numbers that the bosonic field might possess. The creation and annihilation operators for fermions obey anti-commutation relations:

$$\{a_{p\sigma}, a_{p'\sigma'}\} = 0 = \{a_{p\sigma}^\dagger, a_{p'\sigma'}^\dagger\}, \quad \{a_{p\sigma}, a_{p'\sigma'}^\dagger\} = \delta(p-p')\delta_{\sigma\sigma'}.$$

The commutation relations for bosonic creation and annihilation operators reflect the fact that multiple particles associated with a bosonic field can occupy the same state. For the real scalar field $\varphi(x,t)$, this means multiple particles can occupy the same momentum mode p; for bosons with more degrees of freedom, it means that multiple bosons can occupy states with identical quantum numbers. Things are different for fermions: the anti-commutation relations entail that no two particles associated with a fermionic field can occupy the same state, as required by the Pauli exclusion principle.

The Hilbert space $\mathcal{H}$ associated with the free scalar field $\varphi(x,t)$ is the Fock space we just described. How do we represent operators acting on this Hilbert space?

2.2 Operators

The formalism of creation and annihilation operators proves extremely useful here as well. One can prove that *any* operator O acting on $\mathcal{H}$ can be written as a sum of products of creation and annihilation operators (Weinberg, 1995, section 4.2):

$$O = \sum_{N=0}^{\infty} \sum_{M=0}^{\infty} \int dp'_1 \ldots dp'_N \, dp_1 \ldots dp_M \, C_{NM}(p'_1 \ldots p'_N p_1 \ldots p_M)$$
$$\times \, a^{\dagger}_{p'_1} \ldots a^{\dagger}_{p'_N} \, a_{p_M} \ldots a_{p_1},$$

where the C_{NM} are complex-valued coefficients. This means that the action of any operator on states in $\mathcal{H}$ can be described by acting with an appropriate sequence of creation and annihilation operators. (Note that all of the creation operators are to the left of the annihilation operators; this is called *normal ordering*. We will always assume our operators are normal ordered.) It is instructive to see a couple of operators expressed in this form; eventually, we will see how to express the field operators $\varphi(x,t)$ themselves this way.

Suppose one wanted an operator that counted the number of particles present in any state of the field. One can construct such an operator using the creation and annihilation operators as follows. First, we were cavalier about normalization when introducing the action of the creation and annihilation operators Section 2.1. If we are more careful, the action of the creation and annihilation operators is

$$a_{p_j} |p_1^{n_1}, \ldots, p_j^{n_j}, \ldots, p_r^{n_r}\rangle = \sqrt{n_j} \, |p_1^{n_1}, \ldots, p_j^{n_j-1}, \ldots, p_r^{n_r}\rangle$$
$$a^{\dagger}_{p_j} |p_1^{n_1}, \ldots, p_j^{n_j}, \ldots, p_r^{n_r}\rangle = \sqrt{n_j + 1} \, |p_1^{n_1}, \ldots, p_j^{n_j+1}, \ldots, p_r^{n_r}\rangle .$$

The product $a^{\dagger}_{p_j} a_{p_j}$ counts the number of particles occupying the momentum mode p_j:

$$a^{\dagger}_{p_j} a_{p_j} |p_1^{n_1}, \ldots, p_j^{n_j}, \ldots, p_r^{n_r}\rangle = \sqrt{n_j} a^{\dagger}_{p_j} |p_1^{n_1}, \ldots, p_j^{n_j-1}, \ldots, p_r^{n_r}\rangle$$
$$= \sqrt{n_j}\sqrt{n_j - 1 + 1} |p_1^{n_1}, \ldots, p_j^{n_j}, \ldots, p_r^{n_r}\rangle$$
$$= n_j |p_1^{n_1}, \ldots, p_j^{n_j}, \ldots, p_r^{n_r}\rangle,$$

We want our operator to count the number of particles occupying *any* momentum mode, so to construct our operator we integrate over all momentum modes:

$$N = \int d^3p \, a_p^\dagger a_p.$$

The result is the *number operator*, an operator that counts the total number of particles in any state of the field.

A particularly important example is the Hamiltonian of the free scalar field $\varphi(x,t)$. Although more frequently expressed using field operators $\varphi(x,t)$, in a form we will see shortly, it is often convenient to write it using creation and annihilation operators:

$$H = \int d^3p \, E_p a_p^\dagger a_p.$$

This Hamiltonian "counts" the total energy in a state of the free scalar field $\varphi(x,t)$. It does this by counting the total number of particles in each momentum mode, with each term weighted by the energy E_p associated with a particle in that mode. It is easy to verify that the Fock space states

$$|p_1^{n_1}, p_2^{n_2}, \ldots, p_r^{n_r}\rangle$$

are eigenstates of this Hamiltonian, with eigenvalues of the form

$$E = E_{p_1} n_1 + \ldots + E_{p_r} n_r.$$

For a QFT describing free fields, the number operator and the Hamiltonian commute: total particle number is conserved during time evolution. This is only true for free fields; in QFT, interactions can create and annihilate particles. For interacting fields, total energy is still conserved but particle number is not.

We can now turn to quantum fields. Recall that the free real scalar field, being a quantum field, is an assignment of an operator to every point on a spacetime manifold $\mathcal{M}$. The operators $\varphi(x,t)$ assigned to each spacetime point are operators and so, by the theorem cited above, can be expressed using creation and annihilation operators:

$$\varphi(x,t) = \int \widetilde{dp} \, a_p e^{ipx} + a_p^\dagger e^{-ipx},$$

where $\widetilde{dp} \equiv \frac{d^3p}{(2\pi)^3 2E_p}$ is a Lorentz invariant integration measure. (The integral over 3-momentum does not look Lorentz invariant, but it is Srednicki (2007, chapter 3).)

Naively, the physical significance of the field operator $\varphi(x,t)$ is that it can create and annihilate particles of any momentum at the spacetime point (x,t). We will see shortly that this is too naive. Nevertheless, it is true, in a sense, that free field operators act on states to create and annihilate particles and even the too-naive reading can be useful in certain respects. Consider acting on the vacuum with the field operator $\varphi(x,t)$ and projecting out any particular momentum mode k as follows:

$$\langle k|\varphi(x,t)|0\rangle \propto \langle 0|a_k \int \widetilde{dp}\, a_p e^{ipx} + a_p^\dagger e^{-ipx}|0\rangle$$

$$= \int \widetilde{dp}\left[e^{ipx}\langle 0|a_k a_p|0\rangle + e^{-ipx}\langle 0|a_k a_p^\dagger|0\rangle \right] = e^{-ikx}.$$

This suggests that acting on the vacuum with the field operator $\varphi(x,t)$ creates a particle localized at the spatial point x. One can already see one sense in which this is too naive: the particle created "at x" is in an eigenstate of momentum k. What could it mean to create a particle in an eigenstate of momentum that is also localized at a spatial point? In Section 3, we will return to this and other subtleties concerning our (in)ability in QFT to localize particles in any bounded region of spacetime.

Field operators also obey commutation relations. Bosonic fields like $\varphi(x,t)$ obey an analogue of the canonical commutation relations that hold between position and momentum in nonrelativistic quantum mechanics:

$$[\varphi(x,t),\varphi(y,t)] = 0 = [\pi(x,t),\pi(y,t)], \quad [\varphi(x,t),\pi(y,t)] = i\delta^3(x-y),$$

where $\pi(x,t) = \frac{\partial}{\partial t}\varphi(x,t)$ is the canonical momentum associated with the field. For fermionic fields, the field and its associated canonical momentum satisfy analogous anti-commutation relations. In both cases, the commutation relations for the field operators hold if and only if the corresponding commutation relations for the creation and annihilation operators are satisfied. (Note that the canonical momentum is *not* the same thing as the observable corresponding to momentum.)

We wrote the Hamiltonian for the free real scalar field $\varphi(x,t)$ using creation and annihilation operators:

$$H = \int d^3p\, E_p a_p^\dagger a_p.$$

Now that we have constructed the field operators, we can write it in a more common form:

$$H = \frac{1}{2}\int d^3x\, \pi(x)^2 + (\nabla\varphi(x))^2 + m^2\varphi(x)^2,$$

where m is the mass of the particle associated with the field $\varphi(x,t)$. It is a useful exercise to show that the two formulations are equivalent (Srednicki, 2007, chapter 3).

We also require that not only the fields themselves, but also any two operators whatsoever commute when they are localized in spacelike separated regions. That is, suppose that two spacetime points x^μ and y^μ cannot be connected by a light signal. We require that any two operators $O(x^\mu)$ and $O(y^\mu)$ commute; this ensures that actions performed at x^μ cannot influence the statistical distribution of outcomes of measurements of $O(y^\mu)$. More generally, if no light signal can connect any two points in bounded regions of spacetime $\mathcal{O}_1$ and $\mathcal{O}_2$, any two operators localized in those regions will commute. This is called the *microcausality* condition.

The field operators are, in a sense, simply operators like any other. Nevertheless, they play a privileged role in QFT. Quantum fields are not necessarily observables themselves; the real scalar field $\varphi(x,t)$ happens to be Hermitian, but others – complex scalar fields, spinor fields, and so on – are not. However, observables can be constructed out of sums of products of field operators. Furthermore, the field itself is the fundamental dynamical object in the theory, in the sense that the equations of motion (i.e., the Euler-Lagrange equations) of any QFT model describe the dynamical evolution of the fields in that model. Our goal in the remainder of this section is to work up to one of the central uses of QFT in particle physics: the calculation of probability distributions for the outcomes of scattering processes.

2.3 Dynamics

Just as in nonrelativistic quantum mechanics, dynamical evolution in QFT is generated by a Hamiltonian H and is represented by a unitary operator

$$U(\tau) = e^{-iH\tau},$$

where τ is the duration of time that the system is subjected to the conditions described by H. (In practice, one encounters Lagrangians much more frequently than Hamiltonians in QFT. We'll see the virtue of formulating QFT using Lagrangians when we encounter path integrals.) However, while use of the Schrödinger picture of time evolution is common in nonrelativistic quantum mechanics, it is rare in QFT. It is much more common to use either the Heisenberg picture or the interaction picture.

In the Heisenberg picture, states of the system are stationary and the operators evolve in time. In the interaction picture, the total Hamiltonian H is split into a "free" term H_0 and an "interaction" term H_{int} and the time-dependence of the system is distributed across the states and the operators: operators evolve in accord with H_0, while the evolution of states is governed by H_{int}. In our discussion of scattering theory, we will make use of the interaction picture. This is worth noting because Haag's theorem demonstrates that the interaction picture is mathematically ill-defined in QFT, a fact that has generated interesting discussion about how to justify use of the interaction picture; see Earman and Fraser (2006), Duncan (2012, chapter 10.5), and Miller (2018).

In particle physics, very frequently the dynamical setting of interest is scattering theory. (For a clear and careful presentation of assumptions employed by several different formulations of scattering theory, see Duncan (2012, chapter 9). For a historical perspective on how scattering theory became central to QFT, see Blum (2017).) In scattering theory, one aims to model the following situation: a set of widely separated, noninteracting particles in some initial state $|\alpha\rangle$ approach each other, interact and undergo extremely complicated motion for some finite period of time, and then once again become widely separated and noninteracting in some final state $|\beta\rangle$. The initial state $|\alpha\rangle$ and the final state $|\beta\rangle$ are both states in the Fock space $\mathcal{H}$ composed of states of the *free* field; this means they are eigenstates of the free Hamiltonian H_0. The justification for this is the assumption that the particles in these initial and final states are sufficiently widely separated as to be noninteracting.

It is worth pausing to be clear about the meaning of "widely separated." Mathematically, one requires only that the particles be strictly noninteracting when their spatial separation becomes infinite. Philosophers are sometimes alarmed by such infinite idealizations. "The tunnels of particle accelerators are only a few meters wide!" they object. "How could particles possibly become sufficiently separated to justify the assumption that they are non-interacting?" Although there are a number of interesting philosophical issues surrounding the use of idealizations in physics, this particular idealization has a straightforward unpacking: one requires only that the spatial separation between the particles be large compared to the range of the forces by which they interact. Often this can be a surprisingly short distance: in the 1930s, Hideki Yukawa showed that a force mediated by a massive particle decays *exponentially* with the distance between the bodies. This means that bodies have to be *very* close together to experience meaningful interactions due to such a force; a meter is so much larger than the range of such a force that it might as well be infinite. (Justifying this assumption for particles that interact via forces mediated by massless particles, like electromagnetism, requires a more subtle mathematical story, since those forces decay only polynomially with distance. See Strocchi (2013, chapter 6.3) or Duncan (2012, chapter 19.1) for discussion.)

A very important fact about scattering theory is that one does not keep track of the detailed dynamical evolution of the particles. One is interested only in the initial and final states long before and long after the scattering event; the scattering itself is treated as a black box. Aside from specifying the interaction in the Hamiltonian, scattering theory says essentially nothing about the extremely complicated behavior that the particles exhibit while interacting. Instead, one is interested in the following question: Given a quantum field in an initial state $|\alpha\rangle$ and a Hamiltonian H, what is the probability distribution over possible final states $|\beta\rangle$ in which one might find the field after the scattering event?

This information is encoded in an object called the S-matrix. The S-matrix consists of matrix elements of the scattering operator S taken between states in the Fock space $\mathcal{H}$, that is, initial and final states $|\alpha\rangle$ and $|\beta\rangle$. The scattering operator S acts on the initial state $|\alpha\rangle$ to turn it into a "post-scattering" state $S|\alpha\rangle$, and the matrix element

$$\langle\beta|S|\alpha\rangle \equiv S_{\beta\alpha}$$

is the probability amplitude for finding the system in the final state $|\beta\rangle$. (The terms "scattering amplitude" and "S-matrix element" are used interchangeably.) The probability of finding the system in the final state $|\beta\rangle$, given that it began in initial state $|\alpha\rangle$ and its dynamical evolution was governed by S, is calculated using the Born rule:

$$|\langle\beta|S|\alpha\rangle|^2.$$

The S-matrix is an object of central importance in particle physics, and in QFT more generally. (At least, in asymptotically flat spacetimes like Minkowski. In cosmologically relevant spacetimes like those that are asymptotically de Sitter, for instance, one cannot define an S-matrix at all (Witten, 2001; Bousso, 2005).) Much of the remainder of this Element is focused on philosophical challenges posed by the strategies that physicists have developed for calculating S-matrix elements.

The reader may be wondering about the nature of the scattering operator S. Its action on the initial state $|\alpha\rangle$ evidently represents dynamical evolution, so how does it relate to the Hamiltonian H? The short answer is that the scattering operator is constructed by taking early-time and late-time limits of operators that are themselves constructed out of the Hamiltonian H, so that the scattering operator takes a state in the asymptotic past $\tau \rightarrow -\infty$ and dynamically evolves it to a state in the asymptotic future $\tau \rightarrow +\infty$.

A slightly more detailed answer begins by returning to our assumption that the initial and final states of the scattering process describe particles so widely separated that they do not interact (for a genuinely detailed answer, see Duncan (2012, chapter 4.3)). This amounts to the assumption that there is a state of the field $|\Psi\rangle$ in the Hilbert space associated with the *interacting theory* such that at very early times $\tau \ll 0$ its dynamical evolution – determined by the *interacting* Hamiltonian – coincides with the dynamical evolution of some state $|\alpha\rangle$ in the Fock space associated with the *free* theory, governed by the *free* Hamiltonian H_0:

$$\lim_{\tau \ll 0} e^{-iH\tau} |\Psi_\alpha\rangle = e^{-iH_0\tau} |\alpha\rangle .$$

The analogue must be true for very late times

$$\lim_{\tau \gg 0} e^{-iH\tau} |\Psi_\beta\rangle = e^{-iH_0\tau} |\beta\rangle .$$

From here, we can define the unitary operator

$$U(\tau) = e^{iH\tau} e^{-iH_0\tau} .$$

This unitary operator is just a time-evolution operator in the interaction picture that evolves a state from an early time τ to a later $T = 0$:

$$U(T,\tau) = e^{iH_0 T} e^{-iH(T-\tau)} e^{-iH_0\tau} \xrightarrow{T=0} U(0,\tau) = e^{iH\tau} e^{-iH_0\tau} .$$

The scattering operator S is obtained by taking early-time and late-time limits of this time-evolution operator in the interaction picture. By taking those limits, one can define the two operators (typically called Møller operators)

$$U^\pm(\tau) = \lim_{\tau \to \pm\infty} U(\tau).$$

Scattering theory calculates transition amplitudes between states that evolve like eigenstates of the free Hamiltonian H_0 at early times and states that evolve like eigenstates of H_0 at late times. One can then use the fact that the dynamical evolution of states in the full, interacting theory will "coincide" with the evolution of states in the free, noninteracting theory at early and late times as follows:

$$\langle\Psi_\beta | \Psi_\alpha\rangle = \langle\beta| U^+(\tau)^\dagger U^-(\tau) |\alpha\rangle = \langle\beta| U(+\infty, -\infty) |\alpha\rangle.$$

This gives the result that the scattering operator S is a unitary operator that dynamically evolves a state of noninteracting particles $|\alpha\rangle$ from the asymptotic past into a state of noninteracting particles $U(+\infty, -\infty) |\alpha\rangle$ in the asymptotic future.

The fact that the initial and final states come from the Fock space associated with a free theory means that we already know them. They are states of the form

$$\left| (p,\sigma)_1^{n_1}; (p,\sigma)_2^{n_2}; \ldots; (p,\sigma)_r^{n_r} \right\rangle,$$

where σ represents any additional quantum numbers the system may have. That means that a generic S-matrix element has the following form:

$$\left\langle (p',\sigma')_1^{n_1'}; (p',\sigma')_2^{n_2'}; \ldots; (p',\sigma')_q^{n_q'} \middle| S \middle| (p,\sigma)_1^{n_1}; (p,\sigma)_2^{n_2}; \ldots; (p,\sigma)_r^{n_r} \right\rangle.$$

The replacement of n_r with n_q' in the final state reflects the fact that while total energy is conserved during a scattering event in QFT, particle number is not.

The take-home points from this section are the following. A quantum field is an assignment of operators to spacetime points. The possible states of a quantum field form a Hilbert space $\mathcal{H}$. Just like in nonrelativistic quantum mechanics, each physical system is associated with an algebra of operators that act on this Hilbert space. Each of these operators can be expressed as a sum of products of creation and annihilation operators. The field operators are no different: they act on states in $\mathcal{H}$ to create or annihilate particles. One of the most important operators in QFT, the scattering operator S, allows one to calculate the probability amplitude that a state $|\alpha\rangle$ of noninteracting particles prepared in the asymptotic past will evolve into a state $|\beta\rangle$ of noninteracting particles in the asymptotic future. These scattering amplitudes are directly related to the quantities one measures in particle physics experiments, like scattering cross sections and branching ratios.

We now must think more carefully about the notion of "particle" that we have been so far employing rather naively. In the first part of Section 3, we do this by way of addressing another very important topic in more detail: the constraints that Poincaré invariance place on the structure of QFT. We then conclude Section 3 by discussing several well-known oddities of "particles" in QFT.

3 Particles

So far we have spoken about particles in QFT as if the notion is unambiguous: they are excitations of quantum fields whose creation or annihilation in a particular state of a quantum field is represented by the action of the operators $a_p^\dagger$ and a_p. In fact, even a little bit of scrutiny reveals the conceptualization of particles to be subtle. In this section, we will look at two important aspects of the concept of a particle in QFT.

The first is Eugene Wigner's pioneering use of the Poincaré group to analyze possible properties of particles in QFT, which has led to an oft-repeated but rather cryptic slogan that a particle *just is* an "irreducible representation of the Poincaré group." Discussing this allows us to revisit an important topic that received short shrift in the previous section: the consequences of requiring Poincaré invariance for the structure of QFT. Wigner's analysis reflects a beautiful connection between the structure of spacetime and the properties of the particles that can exist in that spacetime. (We restrict to Minkowski spacetime, but this connection between spacetime structure and allowed particles persists in more general settings. That can produce startling results; the irreducible representations of the isometry group of de Sitter spacetime, for example, reveal that de Sitter spacetime can accommodate particles whose properties are not allowed by Minkowski spacetime (see, for example, Baumann et al. (2018, section 2.1–2.2)).)

The second is the fact that particles in QFT cannot be restricted to any bounded region of spacetime: they are nonlocalizable. This conflicts rather dramatically with our intuitions about properties a "particle" ought to have and has generated a lot of interest from philosophers.

3.1 Representations of the Poincaré Group

Recall that the primary empirical constraint imposed by Poincaré invariance is that any two observers related by any combination of spatial rotations, Lorentz boosts, and spacetime translations must agree about probability distributions for the outcomes of scattering experiments. This translates into the mathematical requirement that the S-matrix be invariant under (orthochronous) Lorentz transformations and spacetime translations.

Formally, this requires that S-matrix elements satisfy

$$S_{\beta\alpha} = \langle \beta \,|\, S \,|\, \alpha \rangle = \langle \Lambda\beta \,|\, S \,|\, \Lambda\alpha \rangle = S_{\Lambda\beta, \Lambda\alpha},$$

where $|\Lambda\beta\rangle$ and $|\Lambda\alpha\rangle$ are initial and final states obtained by acting on the states $|\beta\rangle$ and $|\alpha\rangle$ with a Poincaré transformation Λ. Poincaré transformations must be represented as unitary operators acting linearly on the Fock space $\mathcal{H}$ – a fact that will be of central importance momentarily – so we can write this requirement as

$$\langle \beta \,|\, S \,|\, \alpha \rangle = \langle \beta \,|\, U^{\dagger}(\Lambda)\, S\, U(\Lambda) \,|\, \alpha \rangle,$$

from which it follows immediately that $S = U^{\dagger}(\Lambda)\, S\, U(\Lambda)$: the scattering operator S is invariant under Poincaré transformations. This is equivalent to requiring that the action of the scattering operator S on any state $|\Psi\rangle$ of a quantum field commutes with the action of an arbitrary Poincaré transformation $U(\Lambda)$.

We said that Poincaré transformations must be represented by unitary operators acting on $\mathcal{H}$. This follows from two facts: (i) we want the probability distributions our QFT predicts for the outcomes of scattering experiments to be invariant under Poincaré transformations, and (ii) a theorem of Wigner stating that the action of any symmetry group in a quantum theory must be represented by a set of unitary or anti-unitary operators acting linearly on $\mathcal{H}$ (Weinberg, 1995, chapter 2, appendix A). (The anti-unitary operators change the sign of the time coordinate and so these representations are ruled out by the restriction to *orthochronous* Lorentz transformations.) The fact that Poincaré transformations act unitarily on $\mathcal{H}$ entails that they preserve the inner product between states in $\mathcal{H}$:

$$\langle \Psi_{\beta} U^{\dagger}(\Lambda) \,|\, U(\Lambda)\Psi_{\alpha} \rangle = \langle \Psi_{\beta} \,|\, U^{\dagger}(\Lambda)\, U(\Lambda) \,|\, \Psi_{\alpha} \rangle = \langle \Psi_{\beta} \,|\, \Psi_{\alpha} \rangle.$$

This means that the isometries of Minkowski spacetime are also isometries of the Hilbert space $\mathcal{H}$. We also consider only *irreducible* representations, for reasons that will be explained shortly.

The structure of these irreducible unitary representations of the Poincaré group will occupy us for the first portion of this section. (There are many good textbook presentations of this material; in roughly increasing sophistication, see Ryder (1996, chapter 2.7), Coleman (2019, chapter 18), or Weinberg (1995, chapter 2).) Our interest in these representations stems from the fact that they are used to classify the allowed particles in a Poincaré invariant QFT.

Wigner discovered that one can label all possible irreducible unitary representations of the Poincaré group by the eigenvalues of two operators. The first is the operator $P^\mu P_\mu = P^2$, where P^μ is the 4-momentum operator. When acting on a single-particle state $|p, \sigma\rangle$, the eigenvalues of this operator are M^2, where M is the mass of the particle. The second is $W^\mu W_\mu = W^2$, where W^μ is the *Pauli-Lubanski operator*. The eigenvalues of this operator are proportional to J^2, where J is the total spin of the particle.

As is familiar from quantum mechanics, the total spin J of a particle can only take half-integer values: $J = 0, \frac{1}{2}, 1, \frac{3}{2}$, and so on. Thus every irreducible unitary representation of the Poincare group can be labeled by a mass M and a total spin J. In our discussion, we will always assume that $M > 0$, that is, we are considering massive particles. (Extending Wigner's analysis to massless particles involves some important mathematical differences, but no major conceptual surprises.) Note that this already rules out, for example, particles with $J = \frac{1}{3}$ because there is no irreducible representation of the Poincaré group under which the states of such a particle could transform.

It is natural to associate irreducible unitary representations that are labeled by these two eigenvalues with *particles* for the following reason. The two operators P^2 and W^2 are *Casimir operators* of the Poincaré group: they commute with every element of the group. This means that the eigenvalues M^2 and J^2 of those operators are invariant under Poincaré transformations. This already suggests that one might be able to use irreducible representations to classify particles, since the mass and total spin of a particle are themselves invariant under Poincaré transformations. There is no combination of spatial rotations, Lorentz boosts, or spacetime translations that can turn an electron into a spin-1 particle or make its mass anything but 0.511 MeV.

However, it is also the case that specifying the state of a particle requires more information than just its mass and total spin. At minimum, fully specifying the state of the particle will require specifying its momentum. If the particle has total spin $J > 0$, then the state description will also specify the state of its spin along a chosen spatial axis, traditionally the z-axis. These properties are *not* Poincaré invariant: they change under general Poincaré transformations. Furthermore, particles usually possess more properties than mass and spin – electric charge, for example. This fact will be important for how we should understand the slogan that particles "are" irreducible representations of the Poincaré group.

We have restricted to *irreducible* representations. The requirement that our unitary representations of the Poincaré group be irreducible is important for understanding Wigner's classification of particles, so it is worth pausing to get clear on irreducibility.

A (matrix) representation of a Lie group G consists of a set of $n \times n$ matrices that satisfy the algebraic relations that define the Lie algebra associated with the Lie group. In quantum theories, we typically want to represent the action of a group on states of a physical system, that is, on rays in a Hilbert space $\mathcal{H}$. This makes matrix representations especially useful, since the action of the group elements on the physical system is reduced to matrix multiplication. Recall that the action of a linear operator on $\mathcal{H}$ is determined by its action on the states in any basis of $\mathcal{H}$. Let $|\Psi_i\rangle$ be an element of a basis for $\mathcal{H}$. Then the action of the group on $\mathcal{H}$ has the following form:

$$U(g)\,|\Psi_i\rangle = \sum_j U(g)_{ij}\,|\Psi_j\rangle,$$

where $U(g)$ is a unitary matrix that represents the the group element g. The action of $U(g)$ "mixes" the basis states among themselves – each basis state is transformed into a linear combination of other basis states.

This allows us to define irreducibility. A representation of a group G acts irreducibly on a Hilbert space $\mathcal{H}$ if there is no nontrivial subspace of states that is left invariant by the action of the group. Intuitively, this means that if one was allowed to move around in $\mathcal{H}$ using only Poincaré transformations, they would never find themselves trapped in a subspace of $\mathcal{H}$.

A simple example illustrates the idea. Consider a Hilbert space $\mathcal{H}$ with the following two subspaces: one subspace $\mathcal{H}_1$ in which all states take the value $Q = 1$ for some variable Q, and a second subspace $\mathcal{H}_2$ in which all states take the value $Q = 2$. If the action of an arbitrary $U(g)$ only turns states in $\mathcal{H}_1$ into linear combinations of states in $\mathcal{H}_1$ and states in $\mathcal{H}_2$ into linear combinations of states in $\mathcal{H}_2$, then $U(g)$ acts *reducibly* on the full Hilbert space $\mathcal{H} = \mathcal{H}_1 \oplus \mathcal{H}_2$. If one starts in $\mathcal{H}_1$, then one is trapped in $\mathcal{H}_1$, and if one starts in $\mathcal{H}_2$, then one is trapped in $\mathcal{H}_2$. Loosely speaking, a representation of a group G acts irreducibly on a Hilbert space $\mathcal{H}$ if, starting in an arbitrary state $|\Psi\rangle$ in $\mathcal{H}$, one can reach any other state in $\mathcal{H}$ by acting on $|\Psi\rangle$ with elements of G.

Irreducibility matters for Wigner's classification of particles for the follow-ing reason. Suppose that mass and total spin were an exhaustive list of the invariant properties of particles. Then we could label states of a particle by momentum and the value of the spin along the z-axis J_z, which can take values between $-J$ and J. For a particle with $J = 1/2$, for example, a possible state is

$$|\Psi\rangle = |p, J_z = 1/2\rangle .$$

A particle state with momentum p can be transformed into a state of any other momentum p' by Lorentz boosts, and a state with spin $J_z = 1/2$ can be trans-formed into a state of any other spin, along any other axis, by a spatial rotation. All Lorentz transformations can be written as a product of Lorentz boosts and rotations, so for a single particle we should be able to transform any particular state into any other state by Lorentz transformations. If there was a subspace of states in the Hilbert space $\mathcal{H}$ associated with our particle into which we could *not* get our particle by Lorentz transformations, those states must be labeled by properties that (i) are invariant under Poincaré transformations and (ii) differ from properties possessed by our particle. The only possibilities are that the states in that subspace of $\mathcal{H}$ are labeled by different values of M or J than our particle.

Following Wigner's analysis, we know this means those states must trans-form under a different irreducible representation of the Poincaré group than the states of our particle. Since we consider states labeled by distinct masses, or distinct total spins, to be states of distinct types of *particles*, we can conclude that if two sets of states transform under distinct irreducible representations of the Poincaré group then they must be states of distinct particles.

If mass and total spin exhausted the properties of elementary particles, there would be a one-to-one correspondence between particle types and irreducible representations of the Poincaré group: two particles would be distinct if *and only if* they transformed under different irreducible representations. In the real world, of course, particles are labeled by many more properties than just mass and spin, and this complicates the correspondence between particle species and irreducible representations of the Poincaré group. Consider two particles we consider distinct: the electron and the positron. These two particles have the same mass and total spin, so their states transform under the same representa-tion of the Poincaré group. The property that distinguishes the two is the electric charge Q: states of the electron have charge -1 and states of the positron have charge $+1$. Electric charge is a quantity of obvious physical importance, but to which the Poincaré group is blind: an irreducible representation of the Poincaré group acts the same way on states with $\pm q$ as long as those states are labeled by the same mass and total spin. This means that, in the real world, different species of elementary particle are not in one-to-one correspondence with distinct irreducible representations of the Poincaré group. (This is not to say that considering irreducible representations of *all* of the symmetries of the theory is insufficient to distinguish distinct particle species. For example, electrons and positrons *are* associated with distinct irreducible representations of the group U(1), whose irreducible representations are labeled by the value of q. Including U(1) will, roughly speaking, "split" the irreducible representation of the Poincaré group in a way that distinguishes electron states and positron states.)

This returns us, finally, to the question of how one ought to understand the slogan that an elementary particle is an irreducible representation of the Poincaré group. I will make two points. The first is that we should resist the idea that the slogan *entails* any kind of structural realism according to which an elementary particle can be *metaphysically identified* with an irreducible representation of the Poincaré group. (One might prefer structural realism on independent grounds, but the point is that the connection between particles and irreducible representations does not force it on us.) One does encounter the idea that it has this implication in the philosophical literature; see for example, Roberts (2011, section 2) (who does not endorse it) for discussion. One ought to resist this interpretation for at least two reasons. First, for the simple reason that there is an acceptable, less metaphysically extravagant understanding: that the *states* of elementary particles transform under irreducible representations of the Poincaré group, while the particles themselves are material bodies. Second, an irreducible representation of the Poincaré group does not fix enough properties on its own to distinguish any two elementary particles. This seems an insurmountable obstacle to *metaphysically* identifying particular elementary particle types, like electrons or muons, with irreducible representations of the Poincaré group.

The second point builds on this inability to map distinct particle species one-to-one onto distinct irreducible representations of the Poincaré group. It is true that the space of states $\mathcal{H}$ associated with any particular particle transforms under *some* irreducible representation of the Poincaré group. In that sense, the slogan does provide a definition of the *general* notion of a particle: a Hilbert space $\mathcal{H}$ in QFT represents a single type of particle if and only if a representation of the Poincaré group acts irreducibly on $\mathcal{H}$. However, as just mentioned, the association is not strong enough to distinguish any two distinct particle species based solely on the representation theory of the Poincaré group. It is true that *if* two sets of states transform under different representations, *then* they are associated with distinct particle species: the two sets of states must be labled by different mass or total spin. However, the *only if* direction fails:

one cannot infer solely from the fact that two particle species are distinct that they transform in distinct representations. It may be that they are only distinguished by quantum numbers that the Poincaré group does not see, like electric charge. The classification of particles afforded by irreducible representations of the Poincaré group is simply not fine-grained enough to support any conceptual or metaphysical identity between *particular* particle types and *particular* irreducible representations.

Quantum fields have been absent from our discussion of the Poincaré group thus far. Many conclusions of Wigner's analysis of particles applies equally well to fields; in particular, the representation theory of the Poincaré group imposes the same constraints on the allowed quantum fields in Minkowski spacetime that it imposed on particle states. (This is unsurprising, given that "particle state" just describes a state of the associated quantum field in which particle(s) are present.) However, it is worth emphasizing a compelling way of understanding the origin of the transformation rules for the field operators: they are inherited from the transformation rules for the states. The logical structure of this is as follows (see Weinberg (1995, chapter 5)).

We began by requiring that probability distributions for the outcomes of scattering experiments, encoded in an S-matrix, be invariant under Poincaré transformations. This required that Poincaré transformations act unitarily on $\mathcal{H}$. Consider the single particle state

$$|p,\sigma\rangle = a^{\dagger}_{p,\sigma}|0\rangle,$$

where σ represents all quantum numbers of the particle. Acting on this state with a Poincaré transformation $U(\Lambda)$ gives

$$U(\Lambda)|p,\sigma\rangle = U(\Lambda)\,a^{\dagger}_{p,\sigma}\left(U^{\dagger}(\Lambda)\,U(\Lambda)\right)|0\rangle = U(\Lambda)\,a^{\dagger}_{p,\sigma}\,U^{\dagger}(\Lambda)\,|0\rangle,$$

where $U(\Lambda)|0\rangle = |0\rangle$ because the vacuum state $|0\rangle$ does not change under Poincaré transformations. Taking the Hermitian conjugate of this expression gives the transformation rule for the annihilation operator $a_{p,\sigma}$.

The action of the Poincaré transformation on creation and annihilation operators is determined by the mass and total spin of the particle they create or annihilate. Operators for scalar particles, with spin 0, transform differently than operators for vector particles, with spin 1, and both transform differently than spinors, representing particles with spin-1/2. The important point for our purposes is that because quantum fields are constructed out of creation and annihilation operators, the transformation rules for the fields are inherited from the transformation rules for those operators. The simplest example of this is the scalar field: the creation and annihilation operators are the only elements of the field operator on which Poincaré transformations act nontrivially (see

Coleman (2019, chapter 3) for pedagogical discussion of scalar fields and Poincaré transformations). The definition of the scalar field that accompanied us through Section 2 makes this clear, as they are the only operator-valued objects that appear in the definition of the field:

$$\varphi(x,t) = \int \widetilde{dp}\, a_p e^{ipx} + a_p^\dagger e^{-ipx}.$$

The transformation rules for the quantum field is thus determined by the transformation rules for the creation and annihilation operators, which are in turn determined by the transformation rules for the states.

The point of this brief comment about the origin of the transformation rules for fields has been to highlight a fairly direct inferential path that begins with the empirical requirement that probability distributions for the outcomes of scattering experiments be left invariant by Poincaré transformations, passes through the transformation rules for single-particle states, and concludes with the transformation rules for the quantum fields. There are other ways to justify those transformation rules, but this understanding offers a striking demonstration of the powerful constraints placed on the mathematical structure of QFT simply by the empirical need to ensure that the predictions of a quantum theory respect the structure of Minkowski spacetime.

3.2 Localizability

We set out to sharpen our understanding of the concept of a particle in QFT in two ways. The first was to consider its relationship to irreducible representations of the Poincaré group; we have now done that. The second was to consider a serious challenge to our naive use of the term "particle" to describe the content of Fock-space states like

$$\left| (p,\sigma)_1^{n_2};\ (p,\sigma)_2^{n_2};\ \ldots;\ (p,\sigma)_r^{n_r} \right\rangle.$$

It turns out that these "particles" fail to exhibit many of the properties that we would expect particles to exhibit. We will focus on the fact that these "particles" cannot be strictly localized in any bounded region of spacetime, but this is just one of several obstacles to interpreting states of a quantum field as describing particles (both Fraser (2021) and Baker (2016, section 3) include more extensive surveys of these obstacles). We will briefly summarize these other obstacles before turning to the issue of localizability.

The first of these obstacles comes from a remarkable phenomenon called the Unruh effect. (See Mukhanov and Winitzki (2007, chapter 8) for a pedagogical derivation of a special case, Wald (1994, chapter 5) for a more general treatment, and Crispino et al. (2008) for extensive discussion. For philosophical discussion, see Clifton and Halvorson (2001), Arageorgis et al. (2003), Earman (2011), and Ruetsche (2011, chapter 9).) Consider Alice and Bob, both of whom are observing the same free quantum field. Alice is at rest and sees the field in its vacuum state $|0\rangle$, that is, a state containing no particles. The Unruh effect, roughly speaking, is the discovery that if Bob is accelerating uniformly, he will *not* see the field in a no-particle state. Instead, he will see the field in a *thermal state*: a state describing a thermal bath of particles, with a temperature proportional to Bob's rate of acceleration. People have drawn a number of conclusions about the nature of particles from the Unruh effect, but an almost universal reaction has been that it demonstrates that QFT cannot be *fundamentally* about particles. Wald gives a concise statement:

> The Unruh effect may appear paradoxical to readers who are used to thinking that quantum field theory is, fundamentally, a theory of "particles," and that the notion of "particles" has objective significance. How can an accelerating observer assert that "particles" are present [...] when any inertial observer would assert that, "in reality," all of Minkowski spacetime is devoid of particles? ... No paradox arises when one views quantum field theory as, fundamentally, being a theory of local field observables, with the notion of "particles" being introduced as a convenient way of labeling states in certain situations. (Wald, 1994, p. 116)

The second of these obstacles comes from technical issues that arise in defining quantum fields on more exotic spacetimes than Minkowski spacetime (see Wald (1994, chapter 4) or Mukhanov and Winitzki (2007, chapter 6); see Ruetsche (2011, chapters 10–11) for philosophical discussion). In Section 2, the states of the free quantum field that we described as containing particles were Fock states:

$$\left| (p,\sigma)_1^{n_2};\ (p,\sigma)_2^{n_2};\ \ldots;(p,\sigma)_r^{n_r} \right\rangle.$$

We did not discuss it, but the ability to represent states of a quantum field using a Fock space requires the underlying spacetime to possess certain symmetries. The symmetry structure of some curved spacetimes means they do not admit a unique definition of this Fock space representation. This gives rise to multiple, inequivalent representations of the space of states of a free quantum field in those spacetimes, with each representation equipped with its own particle structure. In other curved spacetimes, the symmetry structure means they do not admit any Fock space representation at all. Many have taken the same conceptual lesson from this as from the Unruh effect, which Wald again states clearly:

> [T]his means that there is no natural definition of "particles" in a general, curved spacetime. . . . While some readers familiar with standard presentations of quantum field theory in flat spacetime might be disturbed by the lack of a notion of "particles" in curved spacetime, we have taken great care to emphasize here that this should not be a cause of alarm, since the notion of "particles" plays no essential role in the formulation of quantum field theory. (Wald, 1994, pp. 59–60).

The third obstacle appears if one attempts to extend the particle interpretation of Fock states of a free quantum field to states of *interacting* quantum fields (Fraser, 2008). There are a number of reasons this extension fails. For one, the vacuum state of the interacting quantum fields is not the same as the vacuum state $|0\rangle$ of the free field that was understood to contain zero particles. It is hard to understand how that could be the case if QFTs are fundamentally about particles. Perhaps worse, the single particle state $|p, \sigma\rangle$ is not an eigenstate of the Hamiltonian H_{int} of a QFT that includes interactions. According to one standard approach to property attribution in quantum theories, the fact that the state $|p, \sigma\rangle$ is not an eigenstate of H_{int} means it has no definite value of energy at all. As Fraser argues, this third obstacle poses a serious problem for anyone arguing that QFTs are fundamentally describing particles, or that states of quantum fields always admit a particle description.

These three obstacles pose serious problems for anyone who wants to interpret QFTs as being fundamentally about particles. Indeed, they make it all but impossible to argue even that the states of a quantum field always admit a particle interpretation, even if one abandons the idea that particles are the ontologically fundamental objects. One might wonder whether it is really necessary to take up the issue of localizability as well. Doesn't this coffin already have enough nails?

The previous obstacles all involve, in one way or another, departures from the maximally simple context on which we based our naive talk of particles in Section 2: Minkowski spacetime, inertial observers, and a free scalar field $\varphi(x, t)$ whose states admit a unique Fock space representation. The nonlocalizability of particles presents an obstacle to interpreting states of a quantum field as describing particles even in this context, which seems most friendly to a particle interpretation.

First, the most obvious question: Can one define "particles" that are more localized than momentum eigenstates $|p\rangle$, that is, that are localized at all? The answer is yes. It is both physically and mathematically more responsible to represent initial and final states in scattering theory using wavepackets peaked around some momentum p and some spatial point x with respective spreads Δp and Δx; a Gaussian wavepacket provides a familiar example. One can do scattering theory with wavepackets perfectly well. However, at the typical resolution with which scattering experiments are conducted, the probabilities for the possible outcomes are not sensitive to the detailed spatial structure of the wavepacket and the spread of momenta Δp in the wavepacket is typically much smaller than the momentum of the scattering experiment. This is what licenses the use of momentum eigenstates to approximate the wavepackets. (See Peskin and Schroeder (1995, chapters 4.5, 7.2) and Itzykson and Zuber (1980, chapter 5.1) for discussion; for a more rigorous treatment, see Duncan (2012, chapters 6, 9.2–9.3).) We will continue to use approximations going forward, but emphasize that it is not an essential feature of scattering theory.

Of course, even a Gaussian wavepacket in nonrelativistic quantum mechanics is not strictly localizable in any bounded region of spacetime for more than an instant: it has "tails" that extend out to spatial infinity. However, one might consider it essential to a satisfactory notion of "particle" that it be strictly localizable within some bounded region of spacetime. There are a number of formal results demonstrating that no such notion is allowed in relativistic quantum theories.

The earliest prominent result in the philosophical literature was Malament (1996). Malament asked whether it was possible for a relativistic quantum theory to describe even a single strictly localizable particle. Under physically reasonable assumptions, all of which are satisfied for the initial and final states considered in scattering theory, he demonstrated that no such theory is possible. In more detail, Malament demonstrated the following. Consider two disjoint spatial regions $\mathcal{O}$ and $\mathcal{O}'$ and a single instant t, and assume the following:

- *Localizability*: The probability of finding the particle in both regions $\mathcal{O}$ and $\mathcal{O}'$ at t is 0. Formally, if $P_{\mathcal{O}}$ and $P_{\mathcal{O}'}$ are projection operators that check whether the particle is localized in $\mathcal{O}$ or $\mathcal{O}'$ and return 1 for *yes* and 0 for *no*, we require $P_{\mathcal{O}} P_{\mathcal{O}'} |\Psi\rangle = 0$ for all states $|\Psi\rangle$ of the single particle.
- *Translation Covariance*: There is a unitary representation of the translation subgroup of the Poincaré group defined on the Hilbert space $\mathcal{H}$.
- *Energy Bounded Below*: The Hamiltonian operator H has a lowest eigenvalue, that is, the particle has a ground state.
- *Microcausality*: The measurement of an operator in $\mathcal{O}$ cannot affect the statistics of measurements performed in $\mathcal{O}'$: for any two operators $\mathcal{A}$ and $\mathcal{A}'$ restricted to the regions $\mathcal{O}$ and $\mathcal{O}'$, we require $[\mathcal{A}, \mathcal{A}'] = 0$. In particular, for two projection operators P and P' we have $[P, P'] = 0$.

On the basis of those four assumptions, Malament proves that the probability of detecting the single particle localized in any spatial region $\mathcal{O}$ is 0: given an arbitrary state $|\Psi\rangle$ in $\mathcal{H}$ and any spatial region $\mathcal{O}$, the projection operator P

associated to $\mathcal{O}$ gives $P\,|\Psi\rangle = 0$. Malament's result was subsequently strengthened in several respects by Halvorson and Clifton (2002).

These results are widely described as no-go theorems for particles. However, what they actually demonstrate is that in a relativistic quantum theory, one cannot define a position operator. An intuitive way to see this (glossing over some important mathematical subtleties) is that any Hermitian operator – like a position operator – can always be expressed as a weighted sum of appropriate orthogonal projection operators, and these results show that for any bounded region $\mathcal{O}'$, one cannot define an associated projection operator P' whose value reflects the location of a particle.

A natural question is whether there is a different strategy for defining localized particles in QFT. Perhaps the most natural strategy would be to define number operators $\mathcal{N}$ that count the number of particles in a spatial region $\mathcal{O}$ at any particular instant. After all, a global number operator $\mathcal{N}$ was the tool we used in Section 2 to count the total number of particles in a state of a quantum field. Could a local number operator $\mathcal{N}$ be defined that would count the number of particles in the state of a quantum field in a spatial region $\mathcal{O}$?

The answer is *no*, but the strategy fails because of deep aspects of the structure of QFT. That one cannot even *define* a local number operator $\mathcal{N}$ that counts all and only the particles in the spacetime region $\mathcal{O}$ is a well-known consequence of one of the most remarkable theorems of QFT, the Reeh–Schlieder theorem. (See Witten (2018, section II) for a clear presentation of the theorem and Redhead (1995) and Halvorson (2001) for the difficulty it poses for the notion of a localized particle in QFT.) Substantive discussion of the Reeh–Schlieder theorem is beyond the scope of this Element, but its implications for local number operators are easy to state.

One of the properties we wanted for a total number operator is that, when applied to the vacuum state $|0\rangle$ of a quantum field, we have $\mathcal{N}\,|0\rangle = 0$. After all, the vacuum state is the state of the quantum field with no particles present. We would like the same property to hold for a local number operator $\mathcal{N}$. We immediately encounter the problem: it is a consequence of the Reeh–Schlieder theorem that any operator $\mathcal{A}'$ restricted to a bounded region of spacetime $\mathcal{O}'$ satisfies $\mathcal{A}'\,|0\rangle = 0$ if and only if $\mathcal{A}' = 0$, that is, the operator is the zero operator.

In fact, Halvorson and Clifton (2002, section 6) show that the culprit is a microcausality assumption: the requirement that $[\mathcal{N}, \mathcal{N}'] = 0$ for disjoint regions of spacetime $\mathcal{O}$ and $\mathcal{O}'$. If two operators in disjoint spacetime regions do not commute, then measurements in region $\mathcal{O}$ can superluminally affect the long-run statistics of measurement outcomes in $\mathcal{O}'$; this would allow for superluminal signaling. Indeed, if one attempts to ignore the implication of the Reeh–Schlieder theorem and define local number operators anyway, one quickly finds that two number operators restricted to disjoint spacetime regions do not commute, precisely as Halvorson and Clifton claimed they could not (Duncan, 2012, chapter 6.5).

I said above that a widespread reaction to the results discussed in this section is that particles are not part of the fundamental ontology of QFT. This raises a question that is, to my mind, more pressing: What *is* the status of particles in QFT? After all, experimental physicists design particle accelerators, collect data using particle detectors, and so on. What are those accelerators accelerating? What are the detectors detecting? What notion of "particle" is employed by engineers and experimentalists in designing their detection apparatus, and how can one locate that notion in QFT? We have seen that states of a quantum field cannot always be interpreted as describing particles and even in the restricted contexts in which they can, those "particles" do not behave like one might expect. However, considerations like those just mentioned have led to consensus that there must be *some* role for a notion of nonfundamental particles. (See Fraser (2021, section 21.3) and Baker (2016, section 3) for interpretive options.) What that role is, exactly, strikes me as an interesting and challenging question for those interested in ontological implications of QFT.

One natural response to the obstacles to a fundamental ontology of particles is exemplified by the quotations from Wald: conclude that the ontologically fundamental objects in QFT are quantum fields. Particles are emergent, or approximate, entities in QFT: they are descriptions of certain behaviors of quantum fields that can be usefully deployed in a restricted set of circumstances. This too faces significant obstacles. Baker has shown that the most natural interpretation of QFT along these lines faces many of the same problems as particle interpretations (Baker, 2009) (though Sebens (2022) identifies a potential loophole). Furthermore, the choice of a particular operator-valued field φ is highly nonunique: a large class of fields φ, φ', φ'', ..., each apparently exhibiting quite different structure, can be shown to generate empirically equivalent models. A number of mathematically rigorous results capture aspects of this underdetermination; perhaps the most famous example, proven by Borchers, demonstrates that any two fields φ and φ' that satisfy mild conditions will generate identical S-matrices (Streater and Wightman, 1964, chapter 4.6). This suggests that the structure of a quantum field itself is *in principle* underdetermined by the empirical evidence we can acquire about it. This is a variety of underdetermination that has been notoriously challenging for any would-be scientific realist. The ontological standing of quantum fields is, in my opinion, perhaps the most pressing open question about the metaphysics of QFT.

4 Renormalization

Our discussion of QFT so far has been based almost exclusively on the structure of *noninteracting*, or "free" QFT models. Of course, any model that aims to describe physically interesting behavior, like scattering experiments, has to describe particles that interact with each other. Our discussion so far might strike the reader as useless: How much could we possibly expect to learn from noninteracting models about the structure of more realistic models in which particles interact? Perhaps surprisingly, the answer is "rather a lot," at least in many contexts relevant for modeling particle physics experiments.

In this section, we will extend our discussion to models of QFT in which particles interact. The structure of a particular noninteracting QFT, like the free scalar field $\varphi(x,t)$, provides the basis for a model in which the particles associated with the field $\varphi(x,t)$ *can* interact: one obtains the interacting model as a perturbation of the free model. The addition of interactions enables the calculation of nontrivial S-matrix elements, one of the core concerns of workaday particle physicists. Calculations performed with these perturbative methods have produced the most accurate predictions in the history of experimental science: for example, the use of these methods in quantum electrodynamics to calculate the magnetic moment of the electron produces a prediction that has been verified by experiment to eleven decimal places.

However, this perturbative strategy of using the structure of a non-interacting model as a jumping-off point for calculating the behavior of interacting particles is not without difficulties. Most infamously, one encounters divergent integrals when performing calculations: the calculations seem to predict that the probability of each outcome of a scattering process is infinite. Historically, this led to the development of the renormalization methods that we focus on for the bulk of this section. The mathematical formulation and conceptual justification of renormalization methods underwent a significant evolution between their introduction in the immediate wake of World War II and the late 1970s, the point at which the Standard Model of particle physics had achieved widespread acceptance. The methods that initially were dismissed as misguided or ill-formed by luminaries like Heisenberg and Dirac have now come to be seen as invaluable tools for extracting both empirical predictions and conceptual consequences from QFT.

4.1 Correlation Functions and Path Integrals

The clearest way to illustrate the significance of renormalization methods is to sketch a calculation of an S-matrix element using our perturbative strategy. In fact, there are several ways to carry out such a calculation; in this section, we will introduce a particularly powerful approach that uses *path integral* methods.

Path integral methods have come to be preferred in QFT, not least because of their ability to handle certain technical subtleties of gauge theories like quantum electrodynamics or quantum chromodynamics. We will not need to avail ourselves of the technical power of the framework, but path integral methods also make the physical meaning of renormalization methods particularly clear. (This is especially true for the *renormalization group* (RG) methods that we will discuss in Section 4.3.) It will therefore be useful to develop an understanding of path integrals.

We will stick with the scalar field $\varphi(x,t)$. Our first course of action is to add interactions to the theory's dynamics. We treat this interaction as a small perturbation of the dynamics of the noninteracting theory. We add the term $\lambda \varphi(x,t)^4$ describing the interaction, producing the following Hamiltonian:

$$H = \frac{1}{2} \int d^3x \, \pi(x)^2 + (\nabla \varphi(x))^2 + m^2 \varphi(x)^2 + \frac{\lambda}{4!} \varphi(x)^4,$$

where λ is a real number that satisfies $\lambda \ll 1$. This is essential to our perturbative strategy for studying QFTs with interactions: if $\lambda \gtrsim 1$, our assumption that adding interactions does not dramatically alter the structure of the noninteracting theory is no longer justified.

To emphasize the distinction between the dynamics of the noninteracting theory and the perturbing interaction, one typically splits the Hamiltonian into two terms:

$$H_0 = \frac{1}{2} \int d^3x \, \pi(x)^2 + (\nabla \varphi(x))^2 + m^2 \varphi(x)^2$$

$$H_{int} = \frac{\lambda}{4!} \varphi(x)^4,$$

with the total Hamiltonian for the interacting system being given by $H = H_0 + H_{int}$.

We have described the dynamics of our scalar field using a Hamiltonian operator, but in practice it is much more common to use a Lagrangian operator. (The main reason for this is that verifying Poincaré invariance is much simpler in a Lagrangian formalism than a Hamiltonian formalism, since one has to choose a foliation of spacetime to even write down the Hamiltonian.) The *Lagrangian density* for our interacting scalar field is

$$\mathcal{L} = \frac{1}{2} \partial_\mu \varphi(x,t) \partial^\mu \varphi(x,t) - \frac{m^2}{2} \varphi(x,t)^2 - \frac{\lambda}{4!} \varphi(x,t)^4$$

and the Lagrangian itself is obtained by integrating the Lagrangian density over the entirety of space:

$$L = \int d^3x \, \mathcal{L}.$$

The Lagrangian formalism will be central to our discussion of QFT. Also, for notational simplicity we will start writing $\varphi(x,t) \equiv \varphi$ on occasion.

Path integrals provide a powerful method for the calculation of S-matrix elements, but they do so in a slightly roundabout way. What they enable one to calculate directly is a *time-ordered correlation function*, a very important mathematical object in QFT. Roughly speaking, the correlation function encodes the probability amplitude that if a quantum field is excited out of its vacuum state by the creation of particles localized around spatial points $x_1, x_2, \ldots, x_n$ at time t, the field will be found at a later time t' in a state containing particles localized around spatial points $y_1, y_2, \ldots, y_m$. The *Lehmann–Symanzik–Zimmerman (LSZ) reduction formula* tells us how to systematically relate these correlation functions to scattering amplitudes. Details of the LSZ reduction formula lie outside the scope of this Element (see Coleman (2019, chapter 14) for a lucid exposition), but the important conceptual point is that it reduces calculating S-matrix elements to calculating time-ordered correlation functions. This justifies our focus on the latter.

In fact, we can restrict our attention even further: a very useful result called *Wick's theorem* demonstrates that any time-ordered correlation function involving n particles – a so-called n-point function – can always be written as a sum of products of time-ordered correlation functions involving only two particles – so-called two-point functions or propagators. We will therefore focus on the structure of two-point functions for the moment.

There are important differences between the structure of a propagator for a free QFT and an interacting QFT. We will start with free QFT: when we discuss renormalization, we will see that as long as $\lambda \ll 1$ – the essential assumption of our perturbative strategy – the free propagator serves as a "starting point" of sorts for the propagator in the QFT with interactions. For a free scalar field $\varphi(x,t)$, the two-point function is

$$\langle 0 \mid T\varphi(x,t)\,\varphi(y,t') \mid 0 \rangle,$$

where $|0\rangle$ is the ground state of the *noninteracting* Hamiltonian H_0, that is, $|0\rangle$ is the state of the free field $\varphi(x,t)$ in which no particles are present. The function T is the *time-ordering function*: it cares only about the temporal coordinates t and t' and is defined to be:

$$T\varphi(x,t)\varphi(y,t') = \begin{cases} \varphi(x,t)\varphi(y,t') & t > t' \\ \varphi(y,t')\varphi(x,t) & t' > t \end{cases}.$$

T acts on a product of field operators to arrange the fields localized at the earlier spacetime points on the right.

Why is this mathematical object called a "propagator"? Recall that the free field $\varphi(x, t)$ has the form

$$\varphi(x, t) = \int \widetilde{dp}\, a_p e^{ipx} + a_p^\dagger e^{-ipx},$$

and that its action on the vacuum state $\varphi(x, t)|0\rangle$ produces a state containing a single particle with some momentum p, and localized around the spatial point x at time t. (This isn't strictly true: it describes a wavepacket and technically φ creates a momentum eigenstate. However, we discussed earlier how the two are related in scattering theory.) Similarly, the state $\langle 0|\, \varphi(y, t')$ describes a single particle with some momentum q and localized around the spatial point y at time t'. When we sandwich those two states together, we get a transition amplitude encoding the probability that if, at time t, the quantum field was in a state describing a particle of momentum p localized around x, it will be found at a later time t' in a state describing a particle of momentum q localized around y (or vice versa for t' earlier than t). (Conservation of energy requires that $p = q$ for the free propagator, since no interactions will change the particle's momentum between (x, t) and (y, t').) Speaking loosely, the propagator encodes the probability that a particle initially at spacetime point (x, t) will "propagate" to (y, t').

A simple calculation shows that the propagator for a free scalar field takes the form

$$\langle 0\, |\, T\varphi(x, t)\, \varphi(y, t')\, |\, 0\rangle = \int \frac{d^4 p}{(2\pi)^4} e^{-ip(x-y)} \frac{1}{p^2 - m^2 + i\varepsilon}.$$

One is typically interested in more complicated time-ordered correlation functions that encode the probability that if, at t, a quantum field is in a state describing multiple particles localized around spatial points $x_1, x_2, \ldots, x_n$, it will be found at a later t' in a state containing particles localized around spatial points $y_1, y_2, \ldots, y_m$. (In a free QFT, $m = n$ since there are no interactions to create or annihilate particles.) Wick's theorem lets us decompose these n-point functions into sums of products of two-point functions, that is, propagators, so it is sufficient to focus on those.

We now turn to the *path integral methods* that one typically uses to calculate time-ordered correlation functions. Path integrals were initially introduced into quantum mechanics by Feynman (Feynman, 1948), following up on an earlier idea proposed in an obscure paper by Dirac (Dirac, 1933/2005). Our strategy will be to first develop an understanding of the core ideas of the path integral approach in non-relativistic quantum mechanics by way of a great example due to Feynman himself.

Suppose you have the following problem: a source emits a particle that propagates some distance through space and slams into a detection screen. In between the source and the screen is a wall with two slits, labeled A_1 and A_2. You want to calculate the probability that a particle emitted from the source will be detected at a particular point x on the detection screen. This is easy enough: the particle must pass through either A_1 or A_2 to reach the screen, so the total probability amplitude for the particle being detected at x is the sum of two terms: the amplitude for the particle passing through A_1 and being detected at x, and the amplitude for the particle passing through A_2 and being detected at x. If we represent the probability amplitude for a particle passing through slit A_j and being detected at x as $\mathcal{M}(A_j \to x)$, we can write the total amplitude for detecting the particle at x as

$$\mathcal{M}(x) = \mathcal{M}(A_1 \to x) + \mathcal{M}(A_2 \to x),$$

where the probability of the particle being detected at x is given by $|\mathcal{M}(x)|^2$.

Suppose one adds an additional slit A_3 to the wall. The probability amplitude for detecting the particle at x then becomes

$$\mathcal{M}(x) = \mathcal{M}(A_1 \to x) + \mathcal{M}(A_2 \to x) + \mathcal{M}(A_3 \to x).$$

Now suppose that between the first wall and the detector, one adds a second wall with two slits B_1 and B_2. Reasoning as we just did, the probability amplitude for detecting the particle at x now becomes

$$\mathcal{M}(x) = \mathcal{M}(A_1 \to B_1 \to x) + \mathcal{M}(A_2 \to B_1 \to x) + \mathcal{M}(A_3 \to B_1 \to x)$$
$$+ \mathcal{M}(A_1 \to B_2 \to x) + \mathcal{M}(A_2 \to B_2 \to x) + \mathcal{M}(A_3 \to B_2 \to x).$$

If one adds more walls and more slits in each wall, this increases the number of "paths" $A_i \to B_j \to C_k \to \ldots \to Z_n \to x$ that the particle could take between the source and the point x on the detection screen:

$$\mathcal{M}(x) = \sum_i \sum_j \sum_k \cdots \sum_n \mathcal{M}(A_i \to B_j \to C_k \to \ldots \to Z_n \to x).$$

As one approaches infinitely many walls, each with infinitely many slits, one is eventually left with empty space between the source and the detection screen! At this point, there will be infinitely many "paths" between the source and the point x on the detection screen, and we will have to add up *all* of them to calculate the probability amplitude $\mathcal{M}(x)$. The number of paths has become continuously infinite, so this sum becomes an integral over all paths the particle could take between the source and the detection screen: a path integral.

It is worth sketching this more formally. (See Peskin and Schroeder (1995, chapter 9.1).) Suppose one wants to calculate the probability amplitude for detecting a particle at a spatial point q_D on the detection screen, given that it was emitted from the source at the spatial point q_S at an initial time $t = 0$ and its time evolution during that interval was described by $U(T) = e^{-iHT}$ for some Hamiltonian H. This probability amplitude is

$$\mathcal{M}(q_S \rightarrow q_D) = \langle q_D | e^{-iHT} | q_S \rangle.$$

We can divide the time interval T into N segments of length $T/N = dt$. That lets us split the time evolution operator $U(T)$ into a product of N time evolution operators as follows:

$$U(T) = e^{-iHT} = \underbrace{e^{-iHdt} \, e^{-iHdt} \, \cdots \, e^{-iHdt}}_{N \, \text{copies}}.$$

Between each of these new time evolution operators, we can insert copies of the identity operator $\int dq_j |q_j\rangle \langle q_j|$. (We will use the identity operator expressed in the basis provided by the eigenstates $|q_i\rangle$ of the position operator, but in general one can use any appropriate basis.) Each copy of the identity operator corresponds to inserting a new wall in the example we already discussed, and the fact that each copy of the identity contains continuously many eigenstates of position corresponds to the fact that each "wall" has infinitely many slits.

After making these insertions, we get

$$\mathcal{M}(q_S \rightarrow q_D) = \int dq_a \int dq_b \, \cdots \int dq_N$$
$$\langle q_D | e^{-iHdt} | q_q \rangle \langle q_a | e^{-iHdt} | q_b \rangle \langle q_b | e^{-iHdt} | q_c \rangle \cdots \langle q_N | e^{-iHdt} | q_S \rangle.$$

The final step in this process is to take the limit $N \rightarrow \infty$, which makes the time intervals dt arbitrarily short. In the example above, this corresponds to inserting infinitely many walls between the source and the detection screen (captured by the presence of $N \rightarrow \infty$ copies of the identity operator in the above expression), thereby making the time that the particle spends between walls arbitrarily short. The final result for our probability amplitude $\mathcal{M}(q_S \rightarrow q_D)$, expressed as a path integral, is

$$\mathcal{M}(q_S \rightarrow q_D) = \lim_{N \rightarrow \infty} \int dq_a \int dq_b \, \cdots \int dq_N$$
$$\langle q_D | e^{-iHdt} | q_q \rangle \langle q_a | e^{-iHdt} | q_b \rangle \langle q_b | e^{-iHdt} | q_c \rangle \cdots \langle q_N | e^{-iHdt} | q_S \rangle$$

or, in more elegant form,

$$\mathcal{M}(q_S \rightarrow q_D) = \langle q_D | e^{-iHT} | q_S \rangle = \int \mathcal{D}q(t) \exp\left[i \int_0^T dt \, L[\dot{q}(t), q(t)] \right],$$

where we have defined

$$\mathcal{D}q(t) = \lim_{N\to\infty} \int dq_a \int dq_b \dots \int dq_N$$

and $L[\dot{q}(t), q(t)]$ is the Lagrangian, a mathematical object introduced at the beginning of this section. (For more detail on the apparently remarkable emergence of the Lagrangian in the derivation of the path integral, see Peskin and Schroeder (1995, chapter 9.1).)

The integral of the Lagrangian over time is a quantity called the *action*. It can be written for generic initial and final times t_S and t_D as

$$S = \int_{t_S}^{t_D} dt \, L[\dot{q}(t), q(t)].$$

The action S takes a different value for each path from the source q_S to the point q_D on the detection screen, and integrating over all possible paths ensures they all contribute appropriately to the amplitude $\mathcal{M}(q_S \to q_D)$. If we impose the boundary conditions $q(t_S = 0) = q_S$ and $q(t_D = T) = q_D$, this expression lets us compute the probability amplitude $\mathcal{M}(q_S \to q_D)$ by integrating over all paths that begin at the spacetime point $(q_S, t_S = 0)$ and end at the spacetime point $(q_D, t_D = T)$.

We can use path integrals to compute more than transition amplitudes like $\langle q_D, t_D = T | q_S, t_S = 0 \rangle$. We can also compute matrix elements for products of operators taken between two states: quantities like

$$\langle q_D, t_D = T | Tq(t_2) q(t_1) | q_S, t_S = 0 \rangle,$$

where $Tq(t_2) q(t_1)$ is the time-ordered product of position operators. (The time-dependence of the operators indicates the use of the Heisenberg picture here.) Written as a path integral, this gives us

$$\langle q_D, t_D = T | Tq(t_2) q(t_1) | q_S, t_S = 0 \rangle$$
$$= \int \mathcal{D}q(t) q(t_2) q(t_1) \exp\left[i \int_0^T dt \, L[\dot{q}(t), q(t)]\right].$$

In particular, for any state $|\Psi\rangle$ we can write the *time-ordered expectation value* of any product of operators $\langle \Psi | T O(t_n) \dots O(t_1) | \Psi \rangle$ as a path integral by generalizing the above expression in the obvious way. Of course, if the state in question is the vacuum state $|0\rangle$ and the operators are field operators $\varphi(x_j, t_j)$, the resulting expectation value is just the mathematical object that we have been calling a time-ordered correlation function. Indeed, time-ordered correlation functions are often called *vacuum expectation values* in QFT.

It is worth flagging a philosophically interesting feature of path integrals at this point. One often hears the path integral, presented as I just have, described as an integration over "all possible paths" between two spacetime points. The notion of "possibility" here is subtle. The "paths" that appear in the integral, and contribute to the probability amplitude $\mathcal{M}(q_S \to q_D)$, are (in the mathematical sense) *continuous* but, except for a negligible set of paths, *nowhere differentiable*. This raises a puzzle: the equations of motion that dynamically evolve physical systems through spacetime are differential equations, so "paths" that are nowhere differentiable are apparently nomologically impossible. Why is it necessary to include them in the path integral to calculate the amplitude for the nomologically allowed transition $\mathcal{M}(q_S \to q_D)$ correctly? If these apparently nomologically impossible paths are necessarily part of the *explanans* in any attempt to *explain* measurement outcomes, does that endanger the explanatory power that the path integral formalism is often said to possess? (Several authors have recently considered issues surrounding "counterpossible explanations" in physics in general (Tan, 2019; Wilson, 2021) and (Forgione, 2020) has focused on the path integral formalism in particular.) We do not have space to further explore these questions here, let alone settle them, but they seem to me to warrant further consideration.

We can now extend the path integral formalism to QFT. Happily, essentially all of the conceptual machinery developed in the setting of nonrelativistic quantum mechanics generalizes straightforwardly. (There are serious mathematical obstacles to rigorously defining path integrals in QFT that do not plague path integrals in nonrelativistic quantum mechanics, however.) Recall why we are interested in path integrals in QFT: they provide a very useful way to calculate time-ordered correlation functions, and the LSZ reduction formula tells us that the calculation of an S-matrix element reduces to the calculation of the appropriate time-ordered correlation function. In fact, we are able to express the free propagator as a path integral:

$$\langle 0 \mid T\varphi(x,t)\,\varphi(y,t') \mid 0 \rangle = \int D\varphi \, \varphi(x,t)\,\varphi(y,t') \, \exp[iS[\dot{\varphi},\,\varphi]],$$

where the action S is

$$S[\dot{\varphi},\,\varphi] = \int_t^{t'} dt\, L[\dot{\varphi}(x,t),\,\varphi(x,t)].$$

One is integrating over different sequences of states of the quantum field – "paths" through the Hilbert space $\mathcal{H}$ – that would connect the state of the field $\varphi(x,t)\,|0\rangle$ to the state of the field $\langle 0|\,\varphi(y,t')$. (This was also true of the nonrelativistic path integral; our example just happened to be naturally formulated using position states, which made talk about paths through spacetime intuitive.) In scattering calculations we are interested in the asymptotic past and asymptotic future, so the dt integration runs from $-\infty$ to $+\infty$.

The reader might hope that the hard work of the last few pages is nearing a happy ending: an ability to calculate any correlation function in QFT simply by doing the path integral, plugging the result into the LSZ reduction formula to calculate the associated scattering amplitude, and heading off to tell the experimentalists what to look for. Unfortunately, we confront a much more challenging epistemic situation: the path integral can only be computed exactly in noninteracting QFTs and a few very special interacting models. To calculate time-ordered correlation functions in almost any interacting model – including all models useful in particle physics – we resort to approximation methods.

The most common approximation method is perturbation theory. Our reliance on perturbation theory introduces important limitations on what kind of real-world physics we can describe. The biggest limitation is that we can only use perturbation theory to calculate scattering amplitudes for processes in which all particles interact *weakly*. ("Weakly interacting" here has nothing to do with the weak force.) Recall the Lagrangian density for an interacting scalar field $\varphi(x, t)$ that we encountered at the beginning of this section:

$$\mathcal{L} = \frac{1}{2} \partial_\mu \varphi \partial^\mu \varphi - \frac{m^2}{2} \varphi^2 - \frac{\lambda}{4!} \varphi^4.$$

The term $\lambda \varphi^4$ describes *interactions* between the particles associated with the field $\varphi(x, t)$, and the coupling parameter λ encodes the strength of those interactions. Our reliance on perturbation theory requires that $\lambda \ll 1$: only this justifies treating the addition of a term

$$\mathcal{L}_{int} = \frac{\lambda}{4!} \varphi^4$$

to the free Lagrangian

$$\mathcal{L}_0 = \frac{1}{2} \partial_\mu \varphi \partial^\mu \varphi - \frac{m^2}{2} \varphi^2$$

as a small modification of the structure of the noninteracting QFT described by $\mathcal{L}_0$.

Nature has proven remarkably accommodating of our reliance on perturbation theory: all three forces in the Standard Model of particle physics are weakly coupled. (At least, over a large range of length scales; when we discuss RG methods we will see that the strength of an interaction in QFT need not be the same at all length scales.) Nevertheless, it is a significant restriction.

Reliance on perturbation theory alone also puts limits on what we can learn about the structure of any particular model. Even if a model describes quantum fields whose associated particles interact weakly, there will be interesting structural features of that model that cannot be revealed through analyzing it using perturbation theory. These include topological objects, like instantons and solitons (Shifman, 2012, part I), the presence of "confinement" and other exotic behavior in strongly coupled QFTs (Duncan, 2012, chapter 19.3), and more. (*We* are restricting ourselves to perturbation theory, but it is important not to project that degree of reliance on perturbation theory onto the particle physics community itself: particle physicists have developed a number of very useful nonperturbative strategies for extracting information, as for example, Shifman (2012, Part I) illustrates. The applicability of these strategies is difficult and their successes only partial, however, and perturbation theory remains the primary strategy for calculating things like scattering amplitudes.) The epistemic limits associated with the use of perturbation theory can constrain our ability to characterize the metaphysical implications of any particular model. If we acquire good evidence that a particular model of QFT, like quantum electrodynamics, is likely to give a true description of certain phenomena in our world, we cannot give a full characterization of the structure of that model based on a perturbative analysis alone. Philosophers who want to impute metaphysical structure to the world on the basis of perturbative analysis of models of QFT should remember that any such characterization of their metaphysical consequences will be incomplete.

4.2 Renormalization

In opening this section, I noted that one can learn rather a lot about the structure of an interacting QFT by using the corresponding noninteracting QFT as a starting point for the analysis; that is, by adopting the perturbative strategy just described. I have now noted some epistemic challenges imposed on us by that strategy. However, those are not the most notorious challenges presented by the use of perturbation theory. Those are associated with the appearance of divergent integrals when using perturbation theory to calculate time-ordered correlation functions. Since the LSZ reduction formula tells us how to compute a scattering amplitude from a time-ordered correlation function, taking these divergent integrals at face value would mean that the probability of each possible outcome of a scattering process is infinite. It goes without saying that is an unacceptable result.

It is a decent rule of thumb in physics that if you calculated the value of an observable quantity and got "infinity," either the theory is wrong or you used it incorrectly. The appearance of divergences in perturbation theory is a case of the latter: we imported *too much* structure from the noninteracting QFT into the interacting QFT. Renormalization methods are a corrective: they provide a recipe for modifying the parameters that appear in the noninteracting theory to incorporate the effect of adding interactions. A valuable side effect of this procedure is that it eliminates the divergences that appear when doing perturbation theory, *but renormalization itself has nothing essential to do with the removal of divergences* (Weinberg, 1995, sections 10.3–10.4). This is widely recognized about the RG methods we discuss in the next section, but it is equally true (and less widely recognized) of the "early" renormalization methods that we discuss here and which are still useful in practice.

Recall some basic features of our definition of a noninteracting QFT. We took as our starting point the vacuum state $|0\rangle$, the lowest-energy eigenstate of the *noninteracting* Hamiltonian

$$H_0 = \frac{1}{2} \int d^3x \, \pi^2 + (\nabla\varphi)^2 + m^2\varphi^2.$$

We then defined creation and annihilaton operators $a_p^\dagger$ and a_p by their action on the *noninteracting* vacuum state $|0\rangle$: they create or annihilate single particles of momentum p and mass m. We then constructed our field operator $\varphi(x,t)$ out of those creation and annihilation operators and found that the probability amplitude for a field operator $\varphi(x,t)$ to create a single particle of momentum p and mass m by acting on the *noninteracting* vacuum state $|0\rangle$ is

$$\langle p \, | \, \varphi(x,t) \, | \, 0 \rangle = e^{-ipx}.$$

Adding interaction terms to H_0 produces a different Hamiltonian, with different energy eigenstates. This means that the Hamiltonian $H = H_0 + H_{int}$ has a different vacuum state than the noninteracting theory. It is conventional to label the vacuum state of the interacting theory $|\Omega\rangle$ to distinguish it from the vacuum state $|0\rangle$ of its noninteracting counterpart.

This presents a problem: we cannot assume that operators defined to act on $|0\rangle$ will have the same action when applied to $|\Omega\rangle$. For example, we can no longer expect that $\varphi(x,t)$ will create only a single particle when applied to $|\Omega\rangle$: a particle created around a point x will now excite the state of the field at nearby points due to the presence of interactions, and we must account for the possibility that this will put the field into a state containing *multiple* particles. Furthermore, our fields are now interacting: we have no reason to expect any particular relationship between the parameter m corresponding to the "mass" of a fictitious, noninteracting particle associated with the noninteracting field $\varphi(x,t)$ and the experimentally measured masses of real-world, interacting particles associated with the interacting counterpart of $\varphi(x,t)$. It seems that using a noninteracting QFT as the basis for analysis of an interacting QFT falls apart immediately.

Renormalization methods come to the rescue. In a *renormalizable* QFT, renormalization methods show that by rescaling the field operator(s) and modifying a finite number of parameters, we can reproduce the effect of $\varphi(x,t)$ acting on the free vacuum state $|0\rangle$ to create a single particle of mass m, except that now we have a *renormalized* field operator $\varphi_R(x,t)$ acting on the interacting vacuum state $|\Omega\rangle$ to produce a particle with the *renormalized* mass m_R and whose interactions with the field are determined by the *renormalized* interaction strength λ_R. A very important consequence of these replacements is that divergent integrals that appear if we try to calculate time-ordered correlation functions using φ, m, and λ are rendered convergent if we instead use φ_R, m_R, and λ_R.

It will be useful to introduce new names for familiar objects. The parameters that are not directly related to experimental measurements, like the mass m of a fictitious, noninteracting particle, are now labeled with subscripts

$$\mathcal{L}_0 = \frac{1}{2} \partial_\mu \varphi_0 \partial^\mu \varphi_0 - \frac{m_0^2}{2} \varphi_0^2 - \frac{\lambda_0}{4!} \varphi_0^4.$$

These subscripts indicate that they are unrenormalized, or *bare*, fields and parameters. These parameters describe the properties of a fictitious, noninteracting system; they are unmeasurable free parameters and neither theory nor experiment constrains their values. By contrast, the parameters that are directly related to experimental measurements, like the mass m_R of the real-world particle associated with the interacting field φ_R, are called *renormalized* parameters. Finally, we introduce *counterterms* δm and $\delta\lambda$. These relate the experimentally measureable, renormalized parameters to the fictitious bare parameters:

$$m_R \equiv m + \delta m \qquad \lambda_R \equiv \lambda + \delta\lambda.$$

To see how these renormalizations eliminate divergent integrals in perturbation theory, we must first see how perturbation theory works. Suppose we are interested in calculating this time-ordered correlation function:

$$G^{(4)} \equiv \langle \Omega | \varphi(x_1,t_1)\,\varphi(x_2,t_2)\,\varphi(x_3,t_3)\,\varphi(x_4,t_4) | \Omega \rangle.$$

We know that this can be related to a path integral. However, we also know that we can almost never perform this path integral exactly: we can only calculate this correlation function approximately, using perturbation theory. Schematically, the perturbative approximation of $G^{(4)}$ has the form

$$G^{(4)} \approx \sum_{n=1} \lambda_0^n I_n,$$

where λ_0 is the *bare* interaction strength and the I_n are integrals over momenta of the interacting particles. In general, integrals at leading order (i.e., terms proportional to λ_0) are convergent, while typical integrals at second order and higher diverge. For example, for a real scalar field with an interaction term $H_{int} = \frac{\lambda_0}{4!}\varphi^4$, the leading order integral $I_1 = -i\lambda_0$.

The first divergence occurs in the integral(s) I_2 that appear at second order:

$$I_2 \propto \int_0^\infty d^4p \, \frac{i}{p^2 - m_0^2 + i\varepsilon} \, \frac{i}{(s-p)^2 - m_0^2 + i\varepsilon},$$

where s is a function of the incoming and outgoing momenta of the four scattered particles. (It is one of the "Mandelstam variables" s, t, and u. At second order in the perturbative approximation, an integral of the form I_2 actually contributes three times: once for each Mandelstam variable.) At the high-momentum end of the integral, where p approaches infinity, the other variables become negligible and we have

$$I_2 \approx \int^\infty d^4p \, \frac{1}{p^4} = \ln(p).$$

The function $\ln(p)$ diverges as $p \to \infty$ so this integral is divergent. (If our QFT described a *massless* particle, like a photon, this integral would also diverge as $p \to 0$. This is called an *infrared* divergence Weinberg (1995, chapter 13). These raise important foundational considerations that have received less attention from philosophers than they deserve. Regrettably, space constraints force me to follow suit and set them aside.)

We resolve this problem in two steps. (See Duncan (2012, chapter 17) for a thorough presentation of the machinery of perturbative renormalization.) The first step is *regularization*. As it stands, the integral I_2 is nonsense; we cannot do anything mathematically sensible with it, let alone interpret it physically. Regularization renders the integral I_2 mathematically well-defined so that we can perform meaningful mathematical manipulations.

There are many regularization procedures, and the regularization procedure one chooses is determined by the details of the calculation. Nevertheless, they all instantiate the same general strategy. A regularization procedure introduces a new parameter Λ – a *regulator* – that makes a divergent integral I_k convergent. The integral becomes a function of the regulator $I_k(\Lambda)$. For example, the least sophisticated way to regulate the integral I_2 is to cut off the range of integration over the momentum p at some large, but finite, value Λ. As p approaches Λ, we then have

$$I_2 \approx \int^\Lambda d^4p \, \frac{1}{p^4} = \ln(p).$$

This integral is convergent, but the result will be a logarithmic function of Λ. If one removes the regulator prior to renormalization by taking $\Lambda \to \infty$, the logarithmic divergence of the original integral I_2 is reproduced; this is typical of a good regulator.

Every regularization procedure involves some distortion of the mathematical structure of the QFT; one sacrifices some structural features of the model in the course of a calculation with the hope that they can be resurrected once the calculation is complete. For example, Pauli–Villars regularization, a procedure with a proud historical legacy, introduces into a model new quantum fields corresponding to unphysical "ghost" particles. These ghost particles are automatically incorporated into the perturbative expansion and their contributions make previously divergent integrals I_k finite. However, the ghost particles violate the spin-statistics theorem (fermionic ghost fields have to commute and bosonic ghost fields have to anti-commute) and while its proud legacy stems from its early use in Abelian gauge theories, like quantum electrodynamics, it cannot be extended to *non-Abelian* gauge theories, like quantum chromodynamics. An alternative, very popular method, *dimensional regularization*, treats the spacetime dimension in the integral measure d^4p as a continuous variable and performs the integral in a *noninteger* number of spacetime dimensions $d = 4 - \varepsilon$. This method makes it easy to identify the divergent contributions to integrals I_k (which can be difficult as integrals get complicated) and maintains gauge invariant and (except for the following subtlety with fermions) Poincaré invariant expressions at each step of a calculation. However, it also has difficulty maintaining Poincaré invariance in theories with fermion fields. (The difficulty stems from a technical obstruction to defining mathematical objects in fermionic theories called γ matrices, particularly γ^5, in $d \neq 4$ Collins (1984, chapters 4.6, 13.2).) In general, the choice to use any particular regularization will depend on what structure is crucial to preserve during the course of a calculation and what can be temporarily sacrificed.

Resolving the problem of divergent integrals proceeds in two steps. The second step is *renormalization*. (Like regularization procedures, there are many *renormalization schemes* that are more or less suited to a particular calculation; one can think of their status as roughly akin to different coordinate systems.) This amounts to replacing the fictitious, bare quantities φ_0, m_0, λ_0 with their renormalized counterparts φ_R, m_R, λ_R. This is the step that has sometimes been labeled an ad hoc way to eliminate divergences; even Feynman, who won a Nobel Prize for his contribution to inventing renormalization methods, called them "a method for sweeping [infinities] under the rug." Nevertheless, there is a physical basis for the procedure that goes some way toward dispelling the air of mystery around renormalization.

Consider first the renormalization of the mass $m_0 \to m_R$. The bare mass m_0 was associated with a fictitious particle that propagated freely: the presence of a nonzero field in a given region of spacetime did not affect its propagation at all. Of course, in the real world the particle must interact with *something* to be properly in the domain of physics at all, and these interactions affect its propagation. This manifests as a shift in the mass of the particle from the fictitious mass m_0 to the *renormalized*, or *physical* mass m_R. This is the mass that we actually measure experimentally, since we can never isolate the particle from its accompanying field.

An example illustrates the physical intuition (Coleman, 2019, chapter 10.1). Consider a rigid sphere – a ping-pong ball, for example – of volume V. It is propagating in a perfect fluid of density ρ and zero viscosity. Suppose the "bare" mass of the ping-pong ball is

$$m_0 = \frac{1}{10}\rho V.$$

The bare mass of the ping-pong ball is one-tenth the volume it displaces. A naive calculation using m_0 predicts that if one submerged and released the ping-pong ball, it would accelerate upward at $9g$. This would dramatically exceed the maximum g-force experienced by drivers in Formula 1 races ($\sim 6g$), so something has gone wrong.

The solution is to account for the effect of the interaction with the fluid by *renormalizing* the mass: the effect of the complicated dynamics between the ping-pong ball and the fluid is captured by shifting the mass m_0 to the mass m_R that one would measure if the fluid permeated the universe and the ping-pong ball could never be isolated. (A fish-physicist never measures the mass of an isolated ping-pong ball, but a ping-pong ball that is interacting with the surrounding fluid. The mass m_R is the mass that a fish-physicist would measure.) That produces a *renormalized* mass of

$$m_R = m_0 + \frac{1}{2}\rho V.$$

If we make a reasonable assumption about the respective densities of the ping-pong ball and the fluid, re-doing the calculation with m_R produces a physically sensible result: the ping-pong ball accelerates upward at $3/2g$. The interaction between the particle associated with the field φ and the field itself will likewise shift the mass of the particle from $m_0 \rightarrow m_R$. This is the physical basis for mass renormalization.

In general, the bare mass m_0 and the "shift" δm will be functions of the regulator. If we simply cut off our integration at some momentum Λ, then we have

$$m_R = m_0(\Lambda) + \delta m(\Lambda).$$

This turns out to be important.

We also have to renormalize the field operator φ_0. Recall that one consequence of the definition of φ_0 was that its action on the vacuum state $|0\rangle$ created single particles of mass m_0, and the probability amplitude for the propagation of such a particle from (x, t) to (y, t') was

$$\langle 0 \mid T\varphi(x,t)\,\varphi(y,t') \mid 0 \rangle = \int \frac{d^4p}{(2\pi)^4} e^{-ip(x-y)} \frac{1}{p^2 - m^2 + i\varepsilon}.$$

We would like to modify φ_0 so that it is associated with real-world particles of mass m_R, rather than fictitious particles of mass m_0. This means our modification of φ_0 should ensure that it acts on the vacuum state $|\Omega\rangle$ to create single particles of mass m_R. In particular, we want the propagator to describe the propagation of particles of mass m_R:

$$\langle \Omega \mid T\varphi_R(x,t)\,\varphi_R(y,t') \mid \Omega \rangle = \int \frac{d^4p}{(2\pi)^4} e^{-ip(x-y)} \frac{1}{p^2 - m_R^2 + i\varepsilon}.$$

Remarkably, all of this can be achieved by rescaling the field by a factor Z:

$$\varphi_R = Z^{-1/2}\varphi_0,$$

where Z is a function of the renormalized mass m_R and the regulator Λ.

Before we renormalize the interaction strength λ_0, it will be useful to return to the perturbative approximation of the four-point function that set us down this path. To the second order in the perturbative approximation, we have

$$G^{(4)} \approx \lambda_0 I_1 + \lambda_0^2 I_2 + \mathcal{O}(\lambda_0^3)$$

$$= -i\lambda_0 + i\lambda_0^2\left[\ln\left(\frac{\Lambda^2}{s}\right) + \ln\left(\frac{\Lambda^2}{t}\right) + \ln\left(\frac{\Lambda^2}{u}\right)\right] + \mathcal{O}(\lambda_0^3),$$

where we cut off the momentum integration at Λ, and s, t, and u are Mandelstam variables that are functions of the incoming and outgoing momenta of the scattered particles. The form of this amplitude will be very useful for defining the renormalized interaction strength λ_R.

To renormalize the interaction strength λ_0, we have to determine the value of the renormalized interaction strength λ_R. This is done by extracting the value of the physical, or renormalized, interaction strength λ_R from a scattering experiment. When conducting a scattering experiment, one chooses the momenta of the incoming particles and these will determine the energy scale μ at which the experiment is conducted. Suppose one chooses to measure λ_R at the energy scale

$$s_0 = t_0 = u_0 = \mu^2,$$

where s_0, t_0, and u_0 are appropriate values of the Mandelstam variables. One simply *defines* the renormalized interaction strength as a measurable quantity: the value of the scattering amplitude for this scattering process is

$$-\lambda_R = \lambda_0 I_1 + \lambda_0^2 I_2 + \mathcal{O}(\lambda_0^3)$$

$$= -i\lambda_0 + i\lambda_0^2 \left[\ln\left(\frac{\Lambda^2}{s_0}\right) + \ln\left(\frac{\Lambda^2}{t_0}\right) + \ln\left(\frac{\Lambda^2}{u_0}\right) \right] + \mathcal{O}(\lambda_0^3).$$

We can now give an explicit demonstration of how replacing a bare parameter λ_0 with a renormalized parameter λ_R removes the divergent contribution to integrals appearing in a perturbative approximation. (We said earlier that $\lambda \ll 1$ was an assumption of perturbation theory. In fact, what matters is that $\lambda_R \ll 1$; the bare coupling λ_0 is a free parameter whose value is arbitrary.)

First, invert this identity to get an expression for λ_0 as a function of λ_R:

$$-\lambda_0 = -i\lambda_R - i\lambda_0^2 \left[\ln\left(\frac{\Lambda^2}{s_0}\right) + \ln\left(\frac{\Lambda^2}{t_0}\right) + \ln\left(\frac{\Lambda^2}{u_0}\right) \right] + \mathcal{O}(\lambda_0^3).$$

We can then return to our expression for the amplitude

$$G^{(4)} = -i\lambda_0 + i\lambda_0^2 \left[\ln\left(\frac{\Lambda^2}{s}\right) + \ln\left(\frac{\Lambda^2}{t}\right) + \ln\left(\frac{\Lambda^2}{u}\right) \right] + \mathcal{O}(\lambda_0^3)$$

and iteratively substitute this expression for $-\lambda_0$. The reader can readily verify that the result is

$$G^{(4)} = -i\lambda_R + i\lambda_R^2 \left[\ln\left(\frac{s_0}{s}\right) + \ln\left(\frac{t_0}{t}\right) + \ln\left(\frac{u_0}{u}\right) \right] + \mathcal{O}(\lambda_0^3).$$

The result of replacing λ_0 with the renormalized coupling λ_R is that our result for $G^{(4)}$ no longer depends on the regulator Λ! This should come as a big relief: our choice of any particular value for Λ is arbitrary, and a physical theory's predictions about observable quantities should not depend on the arbitrary choices of theorists. Furthermore, after renormalization we are now free to remove the regulator by taking the limit $\Lambda \to \infty$ without reintroducing any divergences into the perturbative approximation.

Other integrals appear in the perturbative approximation that are rendered convergent by shifting the bare mass m_0 to m_R. Remarkably, *these renormalizations are sufficient*: we can now calculate any scattering amplitude without encountering any divergences. It is crucial to appreciate that one does not need to define different renormalized fields and parameters $\varphi_R', m_R', \lambda_R'$ for each different scattering process: we only need to renormalize the fields and parameters once. The result is that any divergent integral I_k, appearing at *any order* in the perturbative approximation, *for any scattering process whatsoever*, will be rendered convergent by the renormalized fields and parameters φ_R, m_R, and λ_R.

A model like the real scalar field theory described by

$$\mathcal{L}_0 = \frac{1}{2} \partial_\mu \varphi_0 \partial^\mu \varphi_0 - \frac{m_0^2}{2} \varphi_0^2 - \frac{\lambda_0}{4!} \varphi_0^4$$

is *perturbatively renormalizable*. This means that all divergent integrals in the perturbative approximation can be made convergent by a renormalization, or "shift," of finitely many parameters. In this case, those parameters are φ_0, m_0, and λ_0. If integrals with novel divergent structure appear at each order of the perturbative approximation, then a finite number of renormalized parameters will not do the job. Such a QFT is called *perturbatively nonrenormalizable*. (For examples and useful discussion, see Schwartz (2014, chapter 22).) For over two decades after World War II, nonrenormalizable QFTs were considered to be useless at best, and probably meaningless. The belief that only models of QFT that were perturbatively renormalizable made sense became an extremely important methodological principle: a model was to be taken seriously if and only if it was renormalizable.

Importantly, requiring perturbative renormalizability constrains the operators that can appear in a Lagrangian. Operators like φ^2 and φ^4 are allowed, but φ^6, φ^8, φ^{10}, and so on would make the model nonrenormalizable. Renormalizability functioned as a kind of theoretical selection mechanism: it dramatically constrained the class of possible QFTs one needed to consider when doing particle physics, making it methdologically very useful.

There was, however, little understanding of the origins of renormalizability and it seemed incredibly lucky that we could describe so much in particle physics using renormalizable QFTs: quantum electrodynamics, quantum chromodynamics, the Standard Model of particle physics, and many others are all perturbatively renormalizable. However, the particle physics community has undergone a sweeping change in outlook. Nonrenormalizable theories are now thought to be perfectly sensible as long as their application is restricted to a limited set of scales, and the fact that renormalizable QFT models have proven useful for describing the (relatively) low-energy experiments we can perform no longer seems mysterious. Indeed, nonrenormalizable models of QFT will occupy much of our attention for the remainder of the volume. (For a window into older attitudes toward renormalizability, see Weinberg (1977); for a modern (re-)evaluation of its importance, see Weinberg (1995, chapter 12.3).) This change has primarily been driven by the advent of the RG methods that we discuss in the next section.

Let us take stock. We began with a bare Lagrangian, expressed in terms of fictitious bare fields and parameters. We had reason to suspect that those were not the appropriate fields and parameters to represent a real-world interacting theory, but attempted to calculate with it nonetheless. Divergent integrals threatened to make our calculations nonsensical. However, we have seen that using *renormalized* fields and parameters neutralizes this threat: we can calculate anything we want, to any order of the perturbative approximation, without encountering divergent integrals. This leads us to replace the original bare Lagrangian with a renormalized Lagrangian:

$$\mathcal{L}_R = \frac{1}{2}\partial_\mu \varphi_R \partial^\mu \varphi_R - \frac{m_R^2}{2}\varphi_R^2 - \frac{\lambda_R}{4!}\varphi_R^4.$$

We can illuminate the relationship between the two by expressing the renormalized Lagrangian in terms of the *bare* fields and parameters along with a set of "shifts," or *counterterms*:

$$\mathcal{L}_R = \frac{1}{2}Z^{-1}\partial_\mu \varphi_0 \partial^\mu \varphi_0 - \frac{(m_0^2 + \delta m^2)}{2}Z^{-1}\varphi_0^2 - \frac{(\lambda_0 + \delta\lambda)}{4!}Z^{-2}\varphi_0^4.$$

All that renormalization amounts to is a shift of the fictitious fields and parameters appearing in the bare Lagrangian.

Before moving on, we should address an important question: why has renormalization produced consternation over the years? The main reason arises from the way that the bare field(s) and parameters depend on the regulator. We were explicit that the bare mass m_0 and the "shift" term δm depend on the regulator Λ; the same is true of λ_0 and $\delta\lambda$ and the factor Z that renormalizes the bare field φ_0. Once we introduce renormalized fields and parameters, we can remove the regulator by taking $\Lambda \to \infty$ and all observable quantities will remain finite: scattering amplitudes, the physical mass m_R and the physical interaction strength λ_R, and so on. *This is not true of the bare parameters and "shift" terms.* They diverge as $\Lambda \to \infty$, although the differences $m_0 + \delta m$ and $\lambda_0 + \delta\lambda$ remain finite and equal to the renormalized parameters λ_R and m_R.

Some have taken this to mean that renormalization theory claims that the ontology of the world contains infinite quantities. The infinite "bare" mass, for example, would represent the "intrinsic" mass of a particle: the mass it would have if it could be somehow isolated from its associated field. How seriously should one take this as imputing some kind of divergent structure to the physical world? Not at all. Indeed, while there were always confusions embedded in this line of thought about perturbative renormalization, the modern understanding of renormalizability made possible by RG methods renders the entire interpretive issue moot.

4.3 Renormalization Group Methods

There really is no such thing as *the* RG. This is why, for example, a good book titled *Renormalization Group* begins by telling the reader that "the notion of renormalization group is not well defined." The authors believe it is more accurate to think of a "*renormalization group point of view* [that] is a very useful unifying conceptual scheme" (Benfatto and Gallavotti, 1995, chapter 1), and I agree. Rather than *the* RG, there is a set of RG methods: a collection of related, but distinct, mathematical tools and calculational strategies that are grouped together because they implement a single, underlying physical vision of how physical phenomena at different length scales can be related.

The essential physical fact underlying the application of RG methods is that many coarse-grained properties of physical systems are largely independent of many of the fine-grained properties one sees when studying the system at higher resolution. In a sense, this is what makes it possible for us to formulate laws of physics at all without first knowing a complete theory of everything: we can identify quantities like "temperature" and "pressure" and "viscosity" and use them to characterize a fluid, formulate mathematical relationships between them, and use those mathematical relationships to make accurate predictions for measurements of observable quantities of the fluid, all without incorporating any information whatsoever about its molecular constituents or the dynamics governing their behavior. This essential independence of many coarse-grained properties is sometimes called "the autonomy of scales" and its exploitation is the essence of the RG methods we discuss in this section and the effective field theory approach introduced in Section 5.

Renormalization group methods play an indispensable role in modern QFT. (They are also indispensable in classical and quantum statistical physics, particularly the study of critical phenomena (Cardy, 1996; Sachdev, 2011).) They are extremely useful – in some cases essential – for calculating S-matrix elements in perturbation theory. This far from exhausts the calculational value of RG methods, which extends beyond the restricted context of perturbation theory (Delamotte, 2012), but that calculational value is described in many good textbooks and is not our primary interest. Renormalization group methods have garnered attention from philosophers because they offer deep conceptual insight into the structure of QFT. Additionally, they have been shown to offer novel inroads to well-worn topics in the philosophy of science like intertheoretic reduction and emergence, multiple realizability, and scientific realism. Accordingly, our focus will be on conceptual aspects of RG methods.

We still have to get a handle on some basic technical machinery of RG methods before we can consider their philosophical implications. The essential idea of RG methods is the following. In QFT, the coarse-grained properties referred to above are observable quantities measured in scattering experiments at some low energy E – that is, scattering experiments involving incoming particles with momenta p_i all much lower than some very high energy Λ. The very high energy scale Λ is an *ultraviolet cutoff*: it plays a dual role in our discussion. One role is that of suppressing contributions of high-energy variables to low-energy observables, in a sense I will explain. The second role is that of the regulator in perturbative renormalization that cuts off the range of momentum integration in otherwise divergent integrals. However, we now have no interest in taking $\Lambda \to \infty$ at any point in our calculation. Instead, we insist that observable quantities measured in scattering experiments conducted at $E \ll \Lambda$ should be independent of the exact value of Λ.

This lets us set up differential equations of the form

$$\Lambda \frac{d}{d\Lambda} \mathcal{O} = 0,$$

where $\mathcal{O}$ is some observable quantity. In general, $\mathcal{O}$ will be a function of multiple variables: the momenta of the incoming particles, the various masses $m_1, \ldots, m_n$ and interaction strengths $g_1, \ldots, g_n$ in the Lagrangian, and the cutoff Λ. We can solve this differential equation by recognizing that the masses, interaction strengths, and so on which $\mathcal{O}$ depends on are themselves functions of Λ and will change as Λ does. The model's predictions for observables $\mathcal{O}$ can remain fixed only if the parameters on which those observables depend can vary with Λ. The change in those parameters traces out a trajectory through a space in which each point $(m_1, \ldots, m_n, g_1, \ldots, g_n, \Lambda')$ corresponds to a set of values for all parameters appearing in the Lagrangian at some particular value Λ' of the ultraviolet cutoff.

The sketch we have just given most closely reflects the *Wilsonian* RG, developed by Kenneth Wilson (Wilson and Kogut, 1974; Duncan, 2012, chapter 16). In fact, there are at least two "renormalization groups" one encounters in QFT: the Wilsonian RG and the *continuum* RG, and it is the latter that one almost always employs when using perturbation theory to perform calculations. (For textbook discussion, see Schwartz (2014, chapter 23), and for some philosophical analysis of the distinction, see Rivat (2019).) However, the two share many of the same conceptual implications and the Wilsonian RG can illustrate those implications with a certain technical simplicity so we will adopt it going forward, although the distinction will briefly become important when introducing effective field theories in Section 5.

Recall that we are interested in time-ordered correlation functions and that these can be computed from a path integral:

$$\langle \Omega | T\varphi(x_1,t_1) \ldots \varphi(x_n,t_n) | \Omega \rangle = \int D\varphi \, \varphi_1 \ldots \varphi_n \, \exp[iS[\dot{\varphi}, \varphi]].$$

Further recall that, roughly speaking, the path integral "adds up" the probability amplitudes associated with each possible path through the space of possible states of the quantum field connecting the initial state to the final state of interest. We have already seen that if we include states of the field that vary on arbitrarily short wavelengths, that is, describe particles of arbitrarily high momenta, we will encounter divergent integrals in perturbative calculations.

Bearing in mind the "autonomy of scales," we might reason that if we are trying to calculate an observable $\mathcal{O}$ associated with a scattering process at energy $E \ll \Lambda$, our calculation should be able to treat as indistinguishable states of the quantum field that differ only on wavelengths Λ^{-1} without changing the predicted value for $\mathcal{O}$. (Remember: in natural units, lengths have units of inverse energy.)

We can represent "ignoring" very short-wavelength excitations of the quantum field by redefining our quantum field as follows:

$$\varphi(x,t) \rightarrow \varphi_\Lambda(x,t) = \int_{<\Lambda} \varphi(x,t) = \int_{<\Lambda} \widetilde{dp}\, a_p e^{ipx} + a_p^\dagger e^{-ipx}.$$

where $\varphi_\Lambda(x,t)$ can only excite particles of momenta $p < \Lambda$. However, if we want predictions for low-energy observables to remain the same, we incur a cost. This is because although probability amplitudes associated with paths that pass through states of the field containing very short wavelength excitations don't contribute significantly to low-energy observables, they do contribute a little bit. Once we've excluded those short wavelength excitations by imposing an ultraviolet cutoff, we need to incorporate the contribution somehow. We do this by adding *infinitely many* additional operators to the original Lagrangian. This produces a new Lagrangian, describing new fields $\varphi_\Lambda(x,t)$, that makes the same predictions for low-energy observables $\mathcal{O}$ as the original Lagrangian. Formally, we have

$$\mathcal{L}_0 = \frac{1}{2}\partial_\mu \varphi_0 \partial^\mu \varphi_0 - \frac{m_0^2}{2}\varphi_0^2 - \frac{\lambda_0}{4!}\varphi_0^4$$

$$\downarrow$$

$$\mathcal{L}_\Lambda = \frac{1}{2}\partial_\mu \varphi_\Lambda \partial^\mu \varphi_\Lambda - \frac{m(\Lambda)^2}{2}\varphi_\Lambda^2 - \frac{\lambda(\Lambda)}{4!}\varphi_\Lambda^4 + \sum_i g_i(\Lambda)O_i,$$

where the operators O_i are products of the field φ_Λ and its derivatives $\partial_\mu \varphi_\Lambda$ that are consistent with the symmetries of the original theory.

We must pause for a bit of dimensional analysis. The action

$$S[\dot{\varphi}, \varphi] = \int dt\, L[\dot{\varphi}(x,t), \varphi(x,t)] = \int d^4x\, \mathcal{L}[\dot{\varphi}(x,t), \varphi(x,t)]$$

has the same units as $\hbar$; natural units set $\hbar = c = 1$, so $S[\dot{\varphi}, \varphi]$ has to be dimensionless. The integration measure d^4x has dimensions of mass^{-4} so this determines the dimensions of operators and parameters appearing in the Lagrangian: the field φ, the derivative operator ∂_μ, and the mass parameter m each have mass dimension $+1$, while the interaction strength λ is dimensionless.

We noted above that requiring perturbative renormalizability constrains the operators that can appear in a Lagrangian. We can now state the constraint in full generality: a model is perturbatively renormalizable if and only if no operators of mass dimension ≥ 4 appear in the Lagrangian. If a Lagrangian contains even one operator of mass dimension greater than 4, the model is nonrenormalizable.

It is immediately clear that the additional operators O_i that appear in $\mathcal{L}_\Lambda$ all have mass dimension ≥ 5. This means the model is nonrenormalizable, but this will turn out not to be a problem. It also seems to spoil the requirement that the action S_Λ be dimensionless. The solution to this is simple, but has important implications: the parameters $g_i(\Lambda)$ associated with the operators O_i must have mass dimension < 0 to ensure that the product $g_i(\Lambda)O_i$ in the action has the appropriate mass dimensions. We can write $\mathcal{L}_\Lambda$ more explicitly as

$$\mathcal{L}_\Lambda = \frac{1}{2}\partial_\mu \varphi_\Lambda \partial^\mu \varphi_\Lambda - \frac{m(\Lambda)^2}{2}\varphi_\Lambda^2 - \frac{\lambda(\Lambda)}{4!}\varphi_\Lambda^4 + \sum_i \frac{g_i}{\Lambda^{d_i-4}}O_i$$

with the parameters defined at the ultraviolet cutoff scale Λ and d_i the mass dimension of the operator O_i.

What happens if we change the scale at which we have defined the quantities in our Lagrangian? After all, any ultraviolet cutoff Λ is as good as any other Λ' as long as both are much larger than the energy scale E characteristic of our experiments. How does the model described by $\mathcal{L}_\Lambda$ relate to $\mathcal{L}'_\Lambda$? Both models make identical predictions for low-energy observables $\mathcal{O}$. Of course, $\mathcal{L}'_\Lambda$ makes use of the field φ'_Λ. The different value of the ultraviolet cutoff means that $\mathcal{L}'_\Lambda$ is ignoring a different set of short wavelength states in the path integral calculation, so the parameters appearing in $\mathcal{L}'_\Lambda$ incorporate different information and take values different from those in $\mathcal{L}_\Lambda$.

However, RG methods tell us more than that. Suppose that $\Lambda' = \Lambda - d\Lambda$; then the change in each parameter with scale can be captured by a set of differential equations. These are the *beta functions* for those parameters:

$$\Lambda \frac{d}{d\Lambda} g_1(\Lambda) = \beta_1(g_1(\Lambda), g_2(\Lambda), \ldots, g_n(\Lambda), \ldots).$$

The beta functions determine how the parameters in the Lagrangian must change as the ultraviolet cutoff is iteratively lowered $\Lambda \rightarrow \Lambda' \rightarrow \Lambda'' \rightarrow \ldots$ to ensure that the predictions for low-energy observables are unchanged. The mathematical operation of lowering the ultraviolet cutoff $\Lambda \rightarrow \Lambda'$ and packaging the omitted information into the parameters in the Lagrangian is an *RG transformation*. This means that a model with ultraviolet cutoff Λ will describe particles as interacting more strongly (or more weakly) than a model with ultraviolet cutoff Λ', even though both make identical predictions for low-energy observables.

Let us take stock. We began with a QFT that aimed to describe states of a quantum field down to arbitrarily short wavelengths, that is, with no ultraviolet cutoff. We saw that we could impose an ultraviolet cutoff Λ without changing the theory's predictions for low-energy observables. However, our original theory was simple: only two parameters m and λ had nonzero values. Our theory with an ultraviolet cutoff is infinitely complicated by comparison: now *infinitely* many parameters m, λ, g_1, ..., g_n, ... have nonzero values. Furthermore, it seems unremarkable that we can keep a model's predictions for low-energy observables fixed when instituting or changing a cutoff: if those low-energy observables now depend on infinitely many parameters, it seems we could predict for those observables not just the same value as the original model, but *any value whatosever*, simply by an appropriate choice of the values of the infinite set of parameters. It seems we are worse off than where we started.

The situation is much better than that. To see this, it helps to introduce a new concept: *theory space*. Theory space, roughly speaking, is an infinite-dimensional vector space where each axis of the space corresponds to one of the parameters m, λ, g_1, ... and each point in the space – each assignment of values to all the parameters – identifies a particular Lagrangian. The values of the parameters in the Lagrangian with ultraviolet cutoff Λ specify an initial point in theory space, and as one iterates an RG transformation, the cutoff is iteratively lowered $\Lambda \to \Lambda' \to \Lambda'' \to \ldots$ and the compensating changes in the values of the parameters will trace out a continuous trajectory through theory space, as determined by the beta functions. Each point along this trajectory identifies a different Lagrangian, but all of them make identical predictions for the values of low-energy observables.

There are certain special points in theory space: these represent models that are *scale-invariant*. Scale invariance is of great importance in QFT in general and renormalization theory in particular (Coleman, 1985, chapter 3), but what matters for our purposes is that scale-invariant models are *fixed points* of an RG transformation. If we begin at a point $g^* = (m^*, \lambda^*, g_1^*, \ldots)$, which is a fixed point of an RG transformation, then that RG transformation will never move us away from it; iterated RG transformations leave us at the point g^* rather than tracing out a trajectory through theory space. This means that the beta functions for all of the parameters are zero at an RG fixed point:

$$\Lambda \frac{d}{d\Lambda} g_j^*(\Lambda) = 0.$$

We are already familiar with the simplest example of a scale-invariant model: a free scalar field described by the Lagrangian

$$\mathcal{L} = \frac{1}{2}\partial_\mu\varphi\partial^\mu\varphi.$$

At this point in theory space, all the parameters m, λ, g_1, ... are zero and an RG transformation never moves one away from this point. (Fixed points corresponding to free QFTs are called Gaussian fixed points.) However, the physics described by this theory is boring. To describe real-world physics, we consider an arbitrary point in theory space near the noninteracting theory: an arbitrarily chosen point where all of the couplings are nonzero but much smaller than 1. (This reflects our continued reliance on perturbation theory, but the RG behavior we describe is not limited to perturbation theory (Delamotte, 2012, section 2).) The behavior we find explains why we should not worry about the presence of infinitely many parameters in a QFT with an ultraviolet cutoff.

Specifically, we find that all of the parameters $g_1, \ldots, g_n, \ldots$ multiplying operators O_i that we added to the Lagrangian *flow back toward their values at the noninteracting fixed point* as we iteratively lower the ultraviolet cutoff. Since their fixed point values are all zero, this means that these couplings get smaller as we lower the cutoff of the theory. (This is true if one is sufficiently near the Gaussian fixed point, as one must be for perturbation theory to be valid, and can neglect terms beyond leading order when calculating beta functions (Peskin and Schroeder, 1995, chapter 12.1). The nonperturbative behavior of irrelevant parameters is more subtle. In a nonperturbative setting, the low-energy value of an irrelevant coupling becomes a function of *only* the low-energy values of the relevant and marginal parameters in the theory. However, that does not guarantee that irrelevant parameters will be small at low energy; see Schwartz (2014, chapter 23.6) or, for a more general treatment, Weinberg (1995, chapter 12.4).) The operators O_i they multiply thus make negligible contributions to low-energy observables and are labeled *irrelevant*. (As shorthand, one often uses "irrelevant" to refer to the parameters themselves.)

However, we also find that the parameters m and λ that appeared in the original theory *do not* flow back toward their values at the fixed point. As the cutoff of the theory is iteratively lowered, the parameter m gets larger and the parameter λ stays (almost) unchanged. The operators φ^2 and φ^4 are thus called *relevant* and *marginal*, respectively. Just like in the original theory, these operators are what determine the values of low-energy observables. (In fact, a more sophisticated analysis typically reveals that a naively marginal operator is either *marginally relevant* or *marginally irrelevant*: it flows away from, or back toward, its fixed point value λ^*, but very slowly (i.e., logarithmically). The

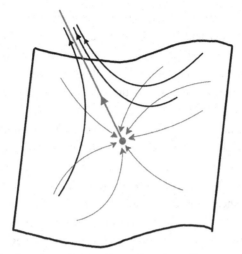

Figure 1 The focusing of RG trajectories. Grey lines are trajectories of irrelevant parameters, dark lines are trajectories of relevant and marginal parameters, and the central line is the trajectory of relevant and marginal operators starting at the critical point

parameter associated with an exactly marginal operator would be unchanged, so its beta function would be zero.)

The flow of the irrelevant parameters back into the fixed point has important consequences. For example, it means that trajectories originating from *any* of the points in theory space near the Gaussian fixed point will quickly focus onto a single trajectory, along which the relevant and marginal parameters flow away from their fixed point values: as the ultraviolet cutoff is iteratively lowered, the differences between the initial points in theory space quickly cease to matter.

What this shows, to use a term familiar to philosophers, is that there is a model

$$\mathcal{L}_U = \frac{1}{2}\partial_\mu\varphi\partial^\mu + m^2\varphi^2 + \lambda\varphi^4$$

whose structure is *multiply realizable*: as the ultraviolet cutoff Λ is lowered, many models that exhibit distinct structure at Λ quickly flow toward the structure exhibited by $\mathcal{L}_U$ as the cutoff is lowered, up to differences suppressed by powers of the ultraviolet cutoff. Physicists have a different name for this multiple realizability: *universality* (Batterman, 2000) (hence the subscript on $\mathcal{L}_U$). In other words, RG methods show that not only low-energy observables but also the low-energy *structure* of QFTs is remarkably insensitive to whatever structure the theory might exhibit at higher energies. This has, understandably, spawned a large literature examining the consequences of universality for questions of intertheoretic reduction and emergence. (See Batterman (2001, 2018, 2019) and Butterfield (2011, 2014) for extensive disussion of two opposing views on how universality bears on reduction and emergence.) Much of this literature has focused on the use of RG methods to analyze critical phenomena in statistical physics, but RG methods and universality raise essentially identical issues in QFT.

This also gives new insight into perturbative renormalizability. Recall that a QFT is perturbatively renormalizable if and only if it includes only relevant and marginal operators, such as φ^2 and φ^4, in its Lagrangian. This analysis explains why restricting to those operators was successful: they are the only operators that make nonnegligible contributions to low-energy observables. Practical limitations mean particle physicists have so far been restricted to experiments at comparatively low energies, so it makes sense that only relevant and marginal operators have been necessary to account for all experimental data. In light of the above RG analysis, then, it no longer seems like incredible luck that so many useful QFT models are renormalizable: it is precisely the relevant and marginal operators that contribute non-negligibly to low-energy observables. (See Polchinski (1984) for the original presentation of this beautiful explanation of renormalizability and Duncan (2012, chapter 17.4) for a textbook discussion.)

Second, it clarifies the significance of taking the limit $\Lambda \to \infty$ when doing perturbative renormalization. Consider a Lagrangian of the form

$$\mathcal{L} = \frac{1}{2}\partial_\mu\varphi\partial^\mu + m^2\varphi^2 + \lambda\varphi^4 + \sum_i \frac{g_i}{\Lambda^{d_i-4}}O_i.$$

As the cutoff is lowered, the irrelevant parameters g_i flow back toward the Gaussian fixed point and the model's predictions approach those of $\mathcal{L}_U$. The parameters in $\mathcal{L}$ trace out a trajectory in theory space that approaches the trajectory on which $\mathcal{L}_U$ lies (the central trajectory in Figure 1). The universal structure of $\mathcal{L}_U$ is captured by the relevant and marginal operators, but $\mathcal{L}$ retains information about the particular theory space trajectory on which it lies: it is encoded in the parameters multiplying the suppressed irrelevant operators. That is, it retains information that distinguishes it from $\mathcal{L}_U$. By taking $\Lambda \to \infty$, we throw away information about the details of this model at the scale of the initial high-energy cutoff, that is, the initial point in theory space from which its RG flow began. Taking $\Lambda \to \infty$ "collapses" all of the RG trajectories in Figure 1 onto the central, attractor trajectory, thereby throwing away any information about the starting points of those trajectories at the scale of the initial cutoff. This is one sense in which the limit $\Lambda \to \infty$ amounts to throwing away information about the high-energy structure of a QFT. (See Delamotte (2012, section 2.6) for additional discussion.)

Renormalization and RG methods are essential to calculating in, and analyzing the structure of, QFT. However, we have not touched on perhaps their most conceptually revolutionary consequence: the reconceptualization of the QFTs used in particle physics as *effective field theories*.

5 Effective Field Theory

In the previous section, we described a phenomenon we called the autonomy of scales: in general, the values of coarse-grained, or low-energy, observable properties of a physical system depend only very weakly (if at all) on the values of many of its fine-grained properties. We can accurately characterize the fine or hyperfine structure of a hydrogen atom without including anything about the properties or state of the constituent quarks of the proton, much like we can characterize the propagation of waves across a stretch of the Pacific Ocean without including anything about the properties or state of the Pacfic's molecular constituents. *Effective field theory* is a way of formulating QFT that exploits this autonomy of scales. (For textbook introductions, see Burgess (2021), Davidson et al. (2020), and Petrov and Blechman (2016); for surveys of select philosophical issues, see Bain (2013) or Rivat and Grinbaum (2020).) Once we identify some phenomena of interest, EFT methods guide the identification of the appropriate variables for characterizing that phenomena, justify writing down dynamical laws in which only those variables appear, and provide a set of techniques for calculating low-energy observables.

The ability of the EFT formalism to identify and calculate with the appropriate variables for characterizing a physical system relies on RG methods. Indeed, Steven Weinberg describes this as their primary virtue:

> [Y]ou are arranging the theory in such a way that only the right degrees of freedom, the ones that are really relevant to you, are appearing in your equations. I think that this in the end is what the renormalization group is all about. It's a way of satisfying the Third Law of Progress in Theoretical Physics, which is that *you may use any degrees of freedom you like to describe a physical system, but if you use the wrong ones, you'll be sorry.* (Weinberg, 1983, p. 16)

This reflects the overlooked fact that explanations of physical phenomena in the EFT framework, by construction, aim to satisfy a desideratum of explanation that has received considerable attention from philosophers: *proportionality*. (It was originally introduced in Yablo (1992) and has received lots of discussion; see, for example, Franklin-Hall (2016), Blanchard (2020), and Woodward (2021a, chapter 8, 2021b) for debate over its formulation and appropriate role in evaluating explanations.) Proportionality constrains the variables one uses to formulate an explanation: roughly speaking, it says one should prefer explanations in which the *explanans* is formulated using variables specified with a degree of detail, or "grain," appropriate for the *explanandum*. A bit more precisely, each *explanans* variable V should be neither so coarsely specified that it omits difference-making information nor so finely specified that it includes irrelevant, or nondifference-making, information.

To take a standard example, suppose a bird always pecks when shown any shade of blue and never pecks when shown any shade of red. Consider two candidate color variables: $C_1 = \{teal, magenta\}$ and $C_2 = \{blue, red\}$. If I show the bird a teal patch and it pecks, which of the following explanations is better: (1) Being presented with a *teal* patch caused the bird to peck (the explanation formulated using C_1), or (2) being presented with a *blue* patch caused the bird to peck (the explanation formulated using C_2)? Proportionality considerations recommend (2). That EFT explanations are constructed to satisfy proportionality constraints – in the sense that they are formulated using variables whose "grain" matches the observables whose values they aim to explain – has not been discussed by philosophers. However, further exploration of the role of proportionality in EFTs promises further insight into their explanatory power. It also brings a novel set of considerations from physical practice to bear on the important (and controversial) question of the appropriate role for proportionality considerations in the analysis of scientific explanation.

We now introduce some basic formal structure of the EFT framework. A caveat: as with our discussion of RG methods, the approach to EFT presented here is the Wilsonian one. In practice one typically encounters continuum EFTs; their formal machinery is somewhat different and they are considerably more efficient for perturbative calculations than the Wilsonian perspective (Georgi, 1993; Manohar, 2020, section 5). Nevertheless, the two perspectives on EFT agree on the essential conceptual matters (though they arguably differ on more peripheral conceptual issues.) We adopt the Wilsonian perspective because it allows for a simpler presentation of these essential conceptual matters.

Happily, we have already done much of the work in our discussion of RG methods. Recall that we showed that to define a QFT with an ultraviolet cutoff Λ, one has to include an infinite number of operators in the Lagrangian: every product of the field φ_Λ and its derivatives $\partial_\mu \varphi_\Lambda$ that is consistent with the symmetries of the original theory. The result is a model of the following form:

$$\mathcal{L}_\Lambda = \frac{1}{2}\partial_\mu\varphi_\Lambda\partial^\mu\varphi_\Lambda - \frac{m(\Lambda)^2}{2}\varphi_\Lambda^2 - \frac{\lambda(\Lambda)}{4!}\varphi_\Lambda^4 + \sum_i \frac{g_i}{\Lambda^{d_i-4}}O_i.$$

The predictions of this model for low-energy observables $\mathcal{O}$ can be held fixed as the value of the ultraviolet cutoff Λ is iteratively lowered by making compensating changes in the parameters m, λ, g_1, ... The change that each parameter undergoes is determined by its beta function

$$\frac{d}{d\Lambda} g_j(\Lambda) = \beta_j(g_1(\Lambda), \ldots, g_n(\Lambda)).$$

We did not really address the physical significance the ultraviolet cutoff. We expect that any QFT model gives an accurate description of nature over only a restricted range of scales. The history of particle physics suggests that as we examine nature at increasingly fine-grained resolution, we should expect to discover novel phenomena that lie beyond the descriptive capacities of the QFT model we used to describe the coarse-grained physics. The original QFT must be supplemented by additional fields (as happened to quantum electrodynamics with the discovery of additional charged leptons, for example), or replaced by a QFT with an entirely novel set of fields and dynamical structure (as happened when quantum chromodynamics was introduced to describe the substructure of baryons and mesons). In either case, the original QFT provided only an *effective* description of physical behavior down to some distance scale Λ^{-1}.

In fact, the entire framework of QFT itself is widely expected to become inapplicable near the Planck scale, the very high-energy scale Λ_{planck} where gravitational interactions between elementary particles become strong. Beyond this scale, the appropriate framework for describing physics is unknown; perhaps it is string theory, perhaps something else. Regardless, we have good reason to believe the framework for describing physics at the Planck scale is not QFT. The ultraviolet cutoff, then, represents a scale beyond which our model cannot be trusted; it reflects our ignorance, or agnosticism, about the appropriate description of nature beyond that scale.

This raises a technical point about the distinction between continuum and Wilsonian EFTs. In Wilsonian EFTs, the ultraviolet cutoff Λ plays a dual role: it regulates divergent integrals in perturbative calculations *and* sets the scale that suppresses the contributions of irrelevant operators to low-energy observables. This is a quirk of Wilsonian EFT: in general, regulating divergent integrals in perturbative calculations is entirely independent of setting the scale that suppresses contributions of high-energy variables to low-energy observables. In continuum EFT, for example, one typically handles divergences in perturbative calculations using dimensional regularization, briefly mentioned above. The scale that suppresses irrelevant operators is chosen independently; the mass M of the lightest particle whose associated field is omitted from the EFT, for example. It is important not to conflate these two distinct roles in the EFT framework.

The type of EFT one constructs when the appropriate variables are known for describing a set of low-energy physical phenomena, but the description of physics above some energy scale Λ is not, is called a *bottom-up* EFT. These play an important methodological role in contemporary particle physics and have many interesting conceptual features. We will return to them after introducing a second type of EFT: a *top-down* EFT.

Top-down EFTs are used when we have a model that includes multiple fields, but are interested in phenomena that depend nonnegligibly on only a subset of those fields. A paradigmatic example is a model describing two scalar fields: a "light" field φ and a "heavy" field χ. The mass m of the particle associated with φ is much smaller than the mass M of the particle associated with χ. Consider the Lagrangian

$$\mathcal{L} = \partial_\mu \varphi \partial^\mu \varphi - m^2 \varphi^2 - \lambda \varphi^4 + \partial_\mu \chi \partial^\mu \chi - m^2 \chi^2 - \lambda \chi^4 - g\varphi^2 \chi^2.$$

Consider a scattering process involving only φ-particles at $E \ll M$: an energy much too low to excite the χ field out of its ground state by creating a χ-particle. We might hope to describe this scattering of φ-particles without including the χ field in our calculation at all.

We are in luck: we can *integrate out* the χ field, removing it from the Lagrangian, *without* affecting scattering amplitudes for energies $E \ll M$. (See for example, Penco (2020, section 2.1) for more details; in continuum EFT, this is accomplished by a procedure called *matching*.) A simple but important object in this model is a particular path integral, the *generating functional*:

$$\langle 0 \mid 0 \rangle_{J_\varphi, J_\chi} = \int D\varphi D\chi \, e^{iS[\varphi, J_\varphi; \chi, J_\chi]}$$

where J_φ and J_χ are *sources*. The generating functional is important because it systematically generates all correlation functions in the theory. To integrate out χ, we split this integration into two parts: an integral over the "heavy" field χ and an integration over the "light" field φ. Schematically, doing the integral over χ produces

$$\langle 0 \mid 0 \rangle_{J_\varphi} = \int D\varphi \, e^{iS_{eff}[\varphi]},$$

where $S_{eff}[\varphi]$ is the *effective action*. It includes only φ and is suitable for calculating scattering amplitudes for any processes involving only φ particles at energies $E \ll M$.

The effective Lagrangian that defines S_{eff} has a now-familiar structure: (i) an ultraviolet cutoff at $\Lambda \sim M$, (ii) an infinite set of irrelevant operators built out of products of $\varphi_{\Lambda\sim M}$ and its derivatives, and (iii) the values of the parameters in the original Lagrangian have been modified and infinitely many new parameters have been introduced, one accompanying each irrelevant operator. (The parameters in an EFT are generically called *Wilson coefficients*.) This EFT produced by integrating out χ cannot be trusted to describe scattering processes at energies $\Lambda \sim M$; scattering at those energies can create χ-particles and the EFT does not have the resources to describe that, by construction. Furthermore, although the canonical use case for integrating out is removing heavy fields from a Lagrangian entirely, integrating out high-energy modes of a field can be useful in a model with only a single field (Duncan, 2012, chapter 16.3).

The irrelevant operators and modified parameters incorporate the small, but nonzero, contributions to φ scattering at $E \ll M$ made by "paths" through the state space of the full theory which pass through states where χ is not in its ground state. That is, the irrelevant operators and modified parameters encode the effects on low-energy observables of high-energy variables (i.e., heavy fields) omitted from our model. This physical significance of irrelevant operators will be important for understanding how bottom-up EFTs are used in particle physics.

We know that these added irrelevant operators appear in the effective Lagrangian suppressed by powers of Λ:

$$\frac{g_n}{\Lambda^{d_n-4}} O_n,$$

where d_n is the mass dimension of the operator O_n. These irrelevant operators encode contributions of omitted heavy fields; their suppression by powers of the cutoff makes precise the sense in which those omitted heavy fields contribute negligibly to low-energy observables, like scattering amplitudes for φ scattering at $E \ll \Lambda$. Dimensional analysis demonstrates that operators O_n with mass dimension $n \geq 5$ make only heavily suppressed contributions to low-energy scattering amplitudes:

$$O_n \sim g_n \left(\frac{E}{\Lambda}\right)^{n-4}.$$

Top-down EFTs isolate the variables that make the dominant contributions to the physical processes one wants to explain; in short, EFTs isolate *difference-making* variables. Furthermore, the explanations they provide in terms of those variables typically satisfy *proportionality* conditions, as discussed above. They also have the practical benefit of simplifying calculations, which often makes the physical meaning of those calculations more transparent. This makes top-down EFTs extremely valuable tools for providing explanations and improving understanding in particle physics.

Bottom-up EFTs have the same formal structure as top-down EFTs but play an expanded role in particle physics. (For introductions to the Standard Model as a bottom-up EFT, see Contino et al. (2016), Henning et al. (2016), and Brivio and Trott (2019).) Bottom-up EFTs are useful when we know the appropriate variables to describe physics at low energies, but – unlike a top-down EFT – we *do not* know the right variables for describing physics at higher energies. A bottom-up EFT is thus formulated using the difference-making variables for observables at energy scales to which we have experimental access, and so exhibits the same explanatory and calculational virtues as a top-down EFT. However, bottom-up EFTs also play an important methodological role in guiding experimental searches for the heavy particles they omit from their description; they function as "engines of discovery" in particle physics. This involves a number of conceptually subtle heuristics (we will discuss several shortly) used to identify scales at which one ought to expect to discover new physics.

We know that the effects of any heavy fields χ omitted from an effective Lagrangian can be captured in the low-energy EFT by adding irrelevant operators, constructed out of products of the light fields and their derivatives, and the values of the parameters. The basic idea of a bottom-up EFT is to imagine that some unspecified heavy fields have been omitted, or integrated out, from our description of low-energy physics. Write down an EFT with the structure that *would have* resulted from actually performing such an integration. That structure is identical to a top-down EFT:

$$\mathcal{L}_\Lambda = \frac{1}{2}\partial_\mu \varphi_\Lambda \partial^\mu \varphi_\Lambda - \frac{m(\Lambda)^2}{2}\varphi_\Lambda^2 - \frac{\lambda(\Lambda)}{4!}\varphi_\Lambda^4 + \sum_i \frac{g_i}{\Lambda^{d_i-4}}O_i.$$

However, there are some important differences. First, in a top-down EFT we know the scale of the ultraviolet cutoff. For a bottom-up EFT, that scale is unknown: we expect there to be *some* scale Λ beyond which our theory cannot be trusted, but that is little guidance. The main functions of the heuristics in the next section is to estimate the scale of the ultraviolet cutoff.

The second difference concerns how bottom-up EFTs are used. One of their most important uses is to probe the unknown heavy fields that have been omitted from our theoretical description, thereby aiding in the search for new physics. Recognizing that irrelevant operators encode effects of omitted heavy fields is essential for understanding how this works. There has been some confusion about this in the philosophical literature, where it has been said that the function of irrelevant operators in EFTs is to preserve the empirical adequacy of an EFT and forestall the need to extend or replace it by adding new fields (e.g.,

Ruetsche (2018)). This is incorrect: their methodological function is precisely to *aid* efforts to extend or replace a bottom-up EFT, not forestall them. Any contribution to an observable from an irrelevant operator in an EFT is "really" a contribution from heavy fields omitted from that EFT.

For instance, consider the SMEFT: the Standard Model as a bottom-up EFT. Consider an extremely simplified situation: there are only two candidate models of beyond the Standard Model physics (BSM). Integrating out the BSM fields in each model at the scale Λ will generate two EFTs with different values of the irrelevant parameters $g_i(\Lambda)$. Suppose that $g_6 = 0$ in one EFT and $g_6 \neq 0$ in the other; then any measured contribution to a low-energy observable made by the operator O_6 immediately rules out the BSM model that produced $g_6 = 0$. (See Henning et al. (2016, section 4) for a more realistic description of this process.) Furthermore, experimentally or theoretically bounding the value of irrelevant parameters can constrain the space of candidate BSM models.

However, recall that we have already seen that many models that give different descriptions of high-energy physics can all exhibit the same low-energy "universal" structure. This makes it hard to constrain the space of candidate BSM models: many different models make very similar predictions for low-energy observables, which makes it challenging to distinguish between these distinct models of the world at short distances if one only has low-energy experimental data. Inconveniently, this is precisely the plight of experimental particle physicists.

Hard, but not impossible. The contributions of BSM models to low-energy observables are typically very small, but not undetectable. One strategy is to perform high-precision measurements of low-energy observables, bounding low-energy observables and thereby constraining the set of candidate BSM models. (See Ellis et al. (2018) for an analysis of current experimental constraints on parameters in the SMEFT and some theoretical implications.) This strategy is indispensable, but also a laborious (and expensive) method for constraining the set of BSM extensions of the Standard Model.

An alternative strategy is to employ various theoretical heuristics to analyze, and constrain, properties of the bottom-up EFTs like the SMEFT. These involve assuming that the model that extends the bottom-up EFT, whatever it may be, satisfies certain generic conditions like unitarity or various causality conditions. One then extracts general constraints that *any* model satisfying those conditions imposes on the bottom-up EFT. This theoretical strategy is a somewhat hot topic in contemporary high-energy physics and is the subject of the next section.

5.1 Discovery Heuristics

It is sometimes said that EFTs "predict their own demise," that is, identify their own limited domain of applicability (e.g., Zee (2010, chapter III.2)). This is true, in a sense. Recall the EFT for a scalar field:

$$\mathcal{L}_\Lambda = \frac{1}{2}\partial_\mu \varphi_\Lambda \partial^\mu \varphi_\Lambda - \frac{m(\Lambda)^2}{2}\varphi_\Lambda^2 - \frac{\lambda(\Lambda)}{4!}\varphi_\Lambda^4 + \sum_i \frac{g_i}{\Lambda^{d_i-4}}O_i,$$

Each operator O_n contributes to amplitudes for scattering at energy E as

$$O_n \sim g_n \left(\frac{E}{\Lambda}\right)^{n-4}.$$

Two consequences of this are worth emphasizing. First, we can estimate the importance of operators for an observable just from its mass dimension: dimension 6 operators contribute more significantly to observables than dimension 8 operators, and so on. This "irrelevance" of irrelevant operators is a core structural feature of EFT and guides the way EFTs are used; for example, analyses of the SMEFT usually focus only on irrelevant operators of mass dimension ≤ 6 because their contributions to low-energy observables are the least suppressed. However, organizing operators this way rests on an assumption about the parameters in the Lagrangian: they are all of approximately $\mathcal{O}(1)$. For example, if the irrelevant parameters g_n can be $\mathcal{O}(\Lambda^2)$ or $\mathcal{O}(\Lambda^4)$, we can no longer estimate the contribution of an operator from its mass dimension alone. This is one form of a *naturalness* assumption, an extremely influential heuristic in high energy physics to which we return momentarily.

Second, for scattering processes at $E \ll \Lambda$, all irrelevant operators make negligible contributions to observables. However, this becomes false as we scatter particles at higher energies; as $E \to \Lambda$ every one of the infinitely many operators O_n in the EFT starts to contribute significantly to observables. Our theory becomes unwieldy to the point of uselessness for describing scattering at energies approaching Λ. Eventually, once $E \sim \Lambda$, the theory begins to predict nonsense: the probabilities for the possible outcomes of a scattering process no longer sum to 1. This would entail that the dynamics of the scattering is not governed by a unitary operator, violating the structure of scattering theory presented in Section 2.

This second point means that an EFT does predict its own demise in the sense that its structure tells us it cannot describe nature at energies near Λ. But what scale is Λ? The structure of the EFT itself tells us nothing on this score. However, the question is very important when using bottom-up EFTs to inform experimental searches for new physics; on its own, the fact that an EFT becomes inapplicable near some finite but otherwise unspecified scale Λ

is of limited use. Do we have theoretical reasons to expect new particles if we conduct experiments at 10 TeV? 100 TeV? What about 500 TeV? These are not idle questions: the answers can lead to decades of labor and billions of dollars spent designing and constructing particle accelerators like the LHC.

We'll begin with naturalness. Since its introduction in the 1970s, naturalness has played an influential role in shaping expectations about the properties of new physics beyond the Standard Model, including the energy scale at which it should be detected. Despite its widespread influence, naturalness involves a number of technical and conceptual subtleties and the justification for them has long been controversial. (For detailed pedagogical presentations, see Cohen (2020, section 3.D) or Penco (2020, section 2.6).) Particle physics research has generated an enormous number of physics papers analyzing and employing naturalness arguments, but questions about its physical interpretation and conceptual status in EFT have recently received increased attention from physicists and philosophers (Giudice, 2013, 2017; Wells, 2015; Williams, 2015, 2019; Borrelli and Castellani, 2019; Rosaler and Harlander, 2019). Those questions have become more pressing with the LHC's ongoing failure to detect any of the new physics predicted by naturalness arguments. Anything from enthusiastic endorsement to extreme skepticism is well-represented in the enormous literature about naturalness; we will sketch only some basics.

Consider a QFT containing a scalar field φ that interacts with a fermion field Ψ:

$$\mathcal{L} = \frac{1}{2}\partial_\mu\varphi\partial^\mu\varphi - \frac{M^2}{2}\varphi^2 - \frac{\lambda}{4!}\varphi^4 + \bar{\Psi}i\gamma^\mu\partial_\mu\Psi - m\bar{\Psi}\Psi + g\varphi\bar{\Psi}\gamma^5\Psi.$$

Suppose $m \gg M$, that is, the fermionic particle is much heavier than the scalar particle. If we scatter φ particles at $E \ll m$, we can describe that scattering using an EFT containing only φ. We integrate out the heavy fermion field and incorporate its contribution to low-energy observables into the parameters and irrelevant operators of the effective Lagrangian. This produces an effective Lagrangian with a cutoff $\Lambda \sim m$. In the EFT, the mass of the scalar particle is shifted to

$$M_R^2 \sim M_0^2 + \Lambda^2 + m^2\left[\ln\left(\frac{\Lambda^2}{m^2}\right)\right].$$

The scalar mass receives additive contributions proportional to m^2 and the cutoff scale Λ^2. (The Λ^2 contribution is an artifact of our regularization method and disappears if we use, for example, dimensional regularization. The m^2 contribution cannot be eliminated this way.) This seems to generate a contradiction: the mass naively attributed to the φ particle in the EFT is larger than the scale $\Lambda \sim m$ at which the EFT becomes inapplicable. That suggests that the "light"

φ particle is somehow too heavy to appear in the EFT that we constructed precisely to describe φ particle scattering!

Recall that the observable, renormalized mass M_R is the sum of a bare mass M_0 and a shift term δM. To resolve the apparent contradiction, the value of the bare mass M_0 of the scalar particle must be finely tuned to precisely cancel the "shift" produced by integrating out the heavy fermion. If this tuning is done correctly, then M_0 and δM sum to the physical mass of the φ particle. This captures one sense in which a light scalar particle is "unnatural": without fine-tuning, the mass of a scalar particle in an EFT is "naturally" on the order of the scale of the ultraviolet cutoff of that EFT.

Renormalization group methods offer additional insight into why many physicists have found this fine-tuning objectionable. Recall that, in *theory space*, each point identifies an EFT defined at a specific cutoff scale Λ with parameter values $m_1, m_2, \ldots, \lambda_1, \lambda_2, \ldots, g_1, g_2, \ldots$. As the cutoff scale is iteratively lowered, the values of the parameters change. This traces out a trajectory through theory space.

Consider an EFT containing multiple particles, with physical masses m_1, m_2, m_3, all heavier than the physical mass M of a scalar particle. (See Barbieri (2013) for a similar discussion.) Define the EFT with an initial cutoff $\Lambda \gg m_1, m_2, m_3$. Every time the ultraviolet cutoff is lowered across one of the mass thresholds $\Lambda' \sim m_i$ and the corresponding field is removed from the EFT, the scalar mass M_R^2 receives a large, quadratic contribution m_i^2. This causes the trajectory through theory space to "jump" across each of these mass thresholds, as the scalar mass is shifted by $\sim m_i^2$.

This means that for the scalar mass M_R^2 to flow to its measured value at experimentally accessible energies $E \ll \Lambda$, the initial point in theory space at the initial cutoff scale Λ must be chosen very precisely: the corrections sustained by scalar mass mean that two initially nearby points in theory space at Λ can flow to points enormously far apart at $\Lambda' \ll \Lambda$. The initial point in theory space at Λ must somehow "know" about the m_i^2 corrections that arise at lower energies and cancel against them in a way that produces the correct measured value of the scalar mass. In many areas of physics, QFT included, one expects parameters in coarse-grained models to be determined by the fine-grained variables being omitted; for example, the values of the parameters in the Navier–Stokes equations used to model the continuum-scale behavior of a fluid are determined by the structure of that fluid at the molecular scale. Many physicists see violations of naturalness as inverting this explanatory order: the value of a low-energy observable, the physical mass of a scalar particle, "determines" structural features of the QFT at higher energies. This perceived inversion of explanatory order is, of course, a common symptom of cases of fine-tuning. Many have also found the extremely sensitive dependence of low-energy observables on the precise values of EFT parameters at much higher energies to violate the expectation of the autonomy of scales.

In particle physics, the most prominent naturalness problem concerns the mass of the Higgs boson, the only elementary scalar particle in nature, and the methodological role of naturalness has been to constrain candidate models of BSM physics. A *natural* extension of the Standard Model is a BSM model that does not require fine-tuning of parameters to generate accurate predictions for measurements of low-energy observables, particularly the mass of the Higgs boson. Each natural BSM model contains some mechanism for eliminating the need for fine-tuning. For example, in BSM models exhibiting supersymmetry (SUSY), a set of heavy particles are postulated whose contributions to the mass of the Higgs boson "naturally" cancel the contributions from the particles in the Standard Model.

This returns us to the use of naturalness to predict the scale Λ bounding the domain of applicability of the Standard Model. SUSY extensions of the Standard Model eliminate any need to fine-tune parameters in the BSM model, but *only* if the new particles aren't too heavy. These particles are not included in the Standard Model, so the mass of the lightest SUSY particle sets the scale Λ for the SMEFT. Other, non-SUSY BSM models propose different mechanisms for eliminating the need for fine-tuning, and these models predict different values for Λ for the SMEFT.

The use of naturalness to constrain BSM models has been extremely influential in particle physics. Accordingly, the LHC's failure to detect any phenomena not completely accounted for by the Standard Model has sent shockwaves through the particle physics community: the most compelling natural extensions of the Standard Model predict new BSM particles with masses in a range that the LHC should have detected. This has led to a methodological crisis in corners of particle physics, with physicists (and philosophers) now considering whether naturalness should be abandoned and what the consequences of doing so would be for how we understand EFT. (One particularly popular line of thinking has emerged according to which naturalness problems are best solved in a *multiverse* setting, of the type produced by models of eternal inflation or the landscape of string theory. For critical discussion, see Giudice (2017) or Williams (2019).)

Naturalness is not the only discovery heuristic in town, thankfully. There is a long (and less contentious) history of exploiting the requirement that the scattering operator S be unitary to estimate the scale Λ at which an EFT becomes inapplicable. These strategies all rely on the fact that in an appropriately chosen region of the complex plane, scattering amplitudes are analytic functions of the scattered particles' momenta. A thorough technical discussion lies beyond the scope of this Element, but we will present the structure of the reasoning in these strategies. (See Schwartz (2014, chapter 24) or Zee (2010, chapter III.8) for pedagogical presentations.)

The heart of these strategies is the optical theorem, which follows from the unitarity of the scattering operator. The optical theorem relates the imaginary part of the amplitude for *forward scattering* – scattering where the final state is the same as the initial state – to the total scattering cross section for all final states. Formally, it states

$$\text{Im}\,\mathcal{M}(i \rightarrow i) \propto \sum_f \sigma(i \rightarrow f),$$

where the scattering cross section $\sigma(i \rightarrow f)$ is a function of the scattering probability $|\mathcal{M}(i \rightarrow f)|^2$. Using the optical theorem, one can derive various bounds on how scattering amplitudes grow as a function of the energy of the scattering process. As an illustration of how such bounds can be used, we will consider the *partial wave unitarity bound*. Employing a useful technique in scattering theory – decomposing a scattering amplitude $\mathcal{M}$ into partial waves indexed by angular momentum j – the amplitude becomes

$$\mathcal{M} = 16\pi \sum_{j=0}^{\infty} a_j(2j+1)P_j(cos\theta),$$

where $P_j(\cos\theta)$ are Legendre polynomials and the a_j are functions of the scattering energy. Employing the optical theorem, we can eventually derive that the coefficients a_j must satisfy

$$|a_j| < 1, \qquad 0 \leq \text{Im}(a_j) \leq 1, \qquad |\,\text{Re}(a_j)| \leq \frac{1}{2}.$$

This bounds how the coefficients a_j – and thus the scattering amplitude $\mathcal{M}$ – can grow with the scattering energy E. Beyond a certain energy scale $E \sim \Lambda$, the coefficients violate the partial wave unitary bound and perturbative calculations of scattering amplitudes in the EFT predict nonsense.

The most important historical application of the partial wave unitarity bound set an upper bound on the Higgs boson mass just as the Standard Model was achieving widespread acceptance in the particle physics community (Lee et al., 1977a, 1977b). They considered the electroweak sector of the Standard Model and examined the scattering of W and Z bosons *without* including a Higgs boson. They found that the scattering amplitudes violated the partial wave unitarity bound at $E \sim 1$ TeV: the electroweak model without a Higgs boson becomes inapplicable at that scale. Furthermore, they showed that the partial wave unitary bound *would* be satisfied if a Higgs boson with mass

$m_H \lesssim 1$ TeV contributed to the scattering amplitude. This offered important insight into the structure of the Standard Model, but perhaps more importantly it served as a discovery heuristic: it gave experimentalists searching for the Higgs boson a bound on the range of energies at which the Higgs boson might be discovered.

Although partial wave unitarity bounds have been useful for estimating the scale at which to search for new physics, they come with caveats. The first is that a violation of a partial unitary bound at some energy Λ actually means one of two things: either some new physics must appear at energies lower than Λ to ensure that scattering amplitudes satisfy the partial wave unitarity bound, *or* the interactions between the fields in the EFT become strong around Λ (i.e., some of the interaction strengths g_i become $\gtrsim 1$). In the latter case, the violation of the partial unitarity bound does *not* indicate that the scattering operator violates unitarity above Λ, but only that the perturbative approximation – premised on the assumption that interactions between particles are weak – becomes unreliable for calculating scattering amplitudes at energies $E \sim \Lambda$. The second caveat is perhaps more serious: there are examples where the scale of new physics – arising either from new physics or strong coupling between fields in the EFT – is not accurately predicted by the scale at which partial wave unitary bounds are violated (Aydemir et al., 2012). This suggests that using the violation of partial wave unitarity bounds in perturbation theory to predict the scale of new physics is at worst unjustified, and at best relies on stronger assumptions about how much information is captured by perturbative approximations than is typically recognized.

The present lack of *experimental* guidance about the scale(s) at which to expect new physics has led particle physicists to develop *theoretical* strategies and heuristics for identifying those scales, and we have touched only two especially prominent ones. Another set of theoretical strategies, popular in contemporary particle physics, proceed by making mild assumptions about the general structure of physics beyond the Standard Model – for example, that whatever the correct BSM model is, it will satisfy certain unitarity, locality, or causality conditions – and then show that any EFT generated from a model satisfying those conditions will exhibit certain generic properties. For example, one can show that certain parameters, or combinations of parameters, in the EFT must be greater than zero; these results are called "positivity bounds." These strategies pursue an epistemic middle ground between bottom-up approaches, where one makes extremely limited assumptions about nature at distances shorter than some cutoff Λ^{-1}, and top-down approach, where one focuses on a specific description of nature at high energies and generates a specific EFT by integrating out heavy fields. (See de Rham et al. (2022) for a recent overview of these strategies with extensive references, Remmen and Rodd (2019) for applications to the SMEFT, and Contino et al. (2016) for clarifying discussion of the "middle-ground" nature of these strategies.) These strategies rely on exploiting conceptually subtle relationships between formal properties, like unitarity or analyticity of scattering amplitudes, and a variety of locality and causality conditions. The analysis of such conditions has long borne fruit for philosophers and careful consideration of these relationships is a promising project for philosophers aiming to engage productively with contemporary particle physics.

5.2 Scientific Realism

A significant amount of philosophical attention has also been devoted to ontological issues in EFTs. Much of that attention has gone to the question of whether EFTs are amenable to scientific realism, that is, whether familiar scientific realist arguments that the best explanation for the predictive success of a theory is that theory's *truth* can be applied to EFTs. The question is pressing because, on the one hand, all predictively successful models of particle physics are EFTs and the core motivation for scientific realism is that it purports to be the best explanation of such predictive successes. On the other hand, EFTs are candidates for neither exact truth nor fundamentality; their predictive accuracy is limited to perturbative approximations of observables measured at energies much lower than some cutoff scale Λ, and they do not even purport to represent nature at distances shorter than Λ^{-1}. These two features mean that an early and enduring understanding of scientific realism – that for a scientific realist, to accept a theory is to accept that it is true (van Fraassen, 1980, chapter 1.1) – is inapplicable to EFTs. They also undermine a widespread norm of theory interpretation: that to give a realist interpretation of a scientific theory is to answer the question, "what must the world be like for this theory to be literally true?" (See Williams (2017, section 2) for related discussion.)

Many have taken this to mean that EFTs are unfit for realist interpretation (Fraser, 2009, 2011; Kuhlmann, 2010; Butterfield and Bouatta, 2015). There is an additional reason one might hold this belief. Effective field theory models accurately represent nature within a restricted domain: an EFT is expected to require modification or replacement to model physics at distances shorter than its cutoff. This suggests that a realist attitude toward EFTs is made a nonstarter by the pessimistic induction: an argument that the history of science suggests that our current successful scientific theories are likely to be modified or replaced in the future, traditionally taken to undermine the realist inference from predictive success to even approximate truth (Laudan, 1981). We can be certain that any EFT model, and perhaps even the entire framework of QFT, will need to be heavily modified or replaced at the Planck length. What justification could we have for being realists about those theories now?

However, recently others have argued that EFT can support more sophisticated, "selective" forms of scientific realism (Williams, 2017; Fraser, 2018, 2020). Selective approaches to scientific realism come in several forms (Worrall, 1989; Kitcher, 1993; Psillos, 1999; Chakravartty, 2007), but their unifying commitment is an attempt to identify realist commitments by answering a more realistic question: "what must the world be like to explain this theory's predictive success?" Different selective realist strategies then propose different strategies for identifying the subset of entities or structural features of the theory that warrant ontological commitment. One common strategy is to identify the entities or structures that play an *essential* role in generating the predictive successes of the theory (e.g., which are indispensable to performing calculations in the theory) and claim that a selective realist ought to be committed only to those.

A long-standing problem for these approaches is that "approximate truth" is notoriously difficult to make precise, raising the worry that a central concept of selective realist approaches must remain unsatisfyingly unclear. In Williams (2017) and Fraser (2018, 2020), it was argued that EFTs provide resources for making approximate truth more precise in that context: the cutoff Λ explicitly delineates the physical domain where the theory can serve as a basis for trustworthy inferences about ontology, and RG methods can be used to identify structural features of an EFT that are universal, that is, that are *stable* or *robust* across a broad range of candidate models for describing nature at distances shorter than Λ^{-1}. (In Williams (2017), it was argued that this was a special case of a general connection between robustness and ontological commitment advocated throughout Wimsatt (2007).) This would yield the optimistic result that inferences about the structure of nature at distances longer than Λ^{-1} that are justified by an EFT's predictive success won't be invalidated when that EFT is eventually embedded in a correct model for describing nature at distances shorter than Λ^{-1}. The enormous predictive success of the Standard Model, for example, can be analyzed to identify the structural features that are essential for those predictions, while RG methods can then be used to determine whether those essential structures are also sufficiently robust that they won't be modified or replaced when we inevitably embed the Standard Model in some as-yet-unknown BSM model. This proposal has come to be called "effective realism."

This strategy faces a number of obstacles. For one, it has been noted that even if the strategy does justify selective realism about certain properties of matter in QFT, it is less clear that the strategy extends to spatiotemporal structure (Ruetsche, 2018, 2020; Chen, 2022; Saatsi, 2022). Additionally, even restricting to properties of matter there is information about quantum fields that cannot be analyzed using the perturbative strategy typically employed when using EFTs in particle physics. This information includes, for example, topological properties of quantum fields like instantons (Weinberg, 1995, chapter 23) and the behavior of strongly interacting fields, such as the quark and gluon fields in QCD at low energies. Even within the domain of applicability of the EFT, perturbation theory offers the realist only partial information, at best, about the nature and structure of reality.

There is a more fundamental obstacle facing the effective realist, however. Even if we grant that suitable norms for realist interpretation can be found for EFTs, and even if we ignore the challenge presented by spatiotemporal structure, the fundamental obstacle is that it is simply unclear that there are any satisfactory candidates for ontological commitment.

In Section 3, we saw that the most natural candidates for ontological commitment in QFT – particles and fields – are, in several respects, unsatisfactory. This situation is unchanged in EFTs. In Fraser (2018), it was proposed that the most natural candidates for ontological commitment are time-ordered correlation functions describing patterns in excitations of a quantum field with wavelengths much longer than Λ^{-1}. (For an intriguingly similar proposal in a distinct physical setting concerning the ontological status of correlation functions, see Batterman (2021).) Renormalization group methods show that these correlation functions are stable across a broad range of candidate models of physics at short distances, making them candidates for ontological commitment. It was argued in Ruetsche (2020) that this would collapse "effective realism" into empiricism, since time-ordered correlation functions can be systematically turned into observable quantities – S-matrix elements – via the LSZ reduction formula. This is uncompelling: time-ordered correlation functions contain considerably more information than is used by the LSZ reduction formula. Roughly speaking, the LSZ reduction formula only cares about the structure of the time-ordered correlation function at the points $p_i^2 = m_i^2$ in momentum space for incoming and outgoing particles. This captures the fact that the S-matrix describes physical states, or "on-shell" states, of the quantum field describing excitations that satisfy the relativistic mass–energy relation $E_p^2 = p^2 + m^2$. However, the time-ordered correlation functions themselves contain additional information about "off-shell" states of the quantum field and this information is necessary for a variety of physical applications beyond scattering theory. It is also the kind of information exploited by foundational mathematical results like the Wightman reconstruction theorem, which allows one to start with a full set of correlation functions and reconstruct the underlying quantum field theory that generated them (Streater and Wightman, 1964, chapter 3.4). Indeed, correlation functions are of fundamental interest especially in contexts where no S-matrix exists, like QFTs in cosmological spacetimes or QFTs with conformal symmetry.

One might alternatively worry that even if, like the structural realists, we accept certain mathematical structures as worthy of ontological commitment, time-ordered correlation functions are not the right sort. Specifically, *ontic* structural realists have identified modal structure as the sort warranting ontological commitment (Ladyman et al., 2007; Esfeld, 2009), and it is far from clear that correlation functions enjoy a comparable modal status to equations of motion, symmetry groups, and other structural commitments that ontic structural realists have advocated. I find it extremely difficult to make sense of unmoored correlation functions, that is, correlation functions that are not understood to describe correlations that obtain between properties of some physical substrate. Any attempt to put this more physical interpretation of the meaning of time-ordered correlation functions on firmer ontological ground immediately returns us to the obstacles we have already encountered in the way of taking the most natural objects – particles or fields – to define the ontology of QFT.

Indeed, it is fitting to conclude with this basic difficulty that has plagued us throughout our attempts to characterize the logical structure, methodological applications, and metaphysical implications of the most predictively successful scientific theories ever constructed: we simply do not have even a satisfactory *candidate* ontology for QFT. We have seen that contemporary particle physics presents us with a diverse set of philosophical puzzles concerning the epistemology and methodological strategies of experimental practice, and for philosophers of physics aiming to make useful contributions to the practice of particle physics these offer a number of promising avenues of inquiry. However, none of these issues cry out for philosophical attention so loudly as the simple question of what QFT is *about*. The fact that we have no entirely satisfactory candidates for the ontology of the most predictively successful scientific theories in history should, by itself, be sufficient to make contemporary particle physics a primary locus of philosophical attention for years to come.

References

Arageorgis, Aristidis, John Earman, and Laura Ruetsche. 2003. Fulling non-uniqueness and the Unruh effect: A primer on some aspects of quantum field theory. *Philosophy of Science*, 70(1):164–202.

Aydemir, Ufuk, Mohamed M Anber, and John F Donoghue. 2012. Self-healing of unitarity in effective field theories and the onset of new physics. *Physical Review D*, 86(1):014025.

Bain, Jonathan. 2013. Effective field theories. In Robert W Batterman, ed., *The Oxford Handbook of Philosophy of Physics*, pages 224–254. Oxford University Press.

Baker, David. 2016. The philosophy of quantum field theory. *Oxford Handbooks Online*. https://academic.oup.com/edited-volume/42642/chapter/358144601. DOI: 10.1093/oxfordhb/9780199935314.013.33.

Baker, David John. 2009. Against field interpretations of quantum field theory. *British Journal for the Philosophy of Science*, 60(3):585–609.

Barbieri, Riccardo. 2013. Electroweak theory after the first LHC phase. *arXiv preprint: 1309.3473*.

Batterman, Robert W. 2000. Multiple realizability and universality. *The British Journal for the Philosophy of Science*, 51(1):115–145.

Batterman, Robert W. 2001. *The Devil in the Details: Asymptotic Reasoning in Explanation, Reduction, and Emergence*. Oxford University Press.

Batterman, Robert W. 2018. Autonomy of theories: An explanatory problem. *Noûs*, 52(4):858–873.

Batterman, Robert W. 2019. Universality and RG explanations. *Perspectives on Science*, 27(1):26–47.

Batterman, Robert W. 2021. *A Middle Way: A Non-Fundamental Approach to Many-Body Physics*. Oxford University Press.

Baumann, Daniel, Garrett Goon, Hayden Lee, and Guilherme L Pimentel. 2018. Partially massless fields during inflation. *Journal of High Energy Physics*. https://doi.org/10.1007/JHEP04(2018)140.

Benfatto, Giuseppe, and Giovanni Gallavotti. 1995. *Renormalization Group*. Princeton University Press.

Blanchard, Thomas. 2020. Explanatory abstraction and the goldilocks problem: Interventionism gets things just right. *The British Journal for the Philosophy of Science*, 71: 633–663.

Blum, Alexander S. 2017. The state is not abolished, it withers away: How quantum field theory became a theory of scattering. *Studies in History and Philosophy of Science Part B: Studies in History and Philosophy of Modern Physics*, 60: 46–80.

Borrelli, Arianna, and Elena Castellani. 2019. The practice of naturalness: A historical-philosophical perspective. *Foundations of Physics*, 49(9): 860–878.

Bousso, Raphael. 2005. Cosmology and the S matrix. *Physical Review D*, 71 (6):064024.

Boyd, Nora Mills. 2021. *Epistemology of Experimental Physics* (Elements in the Philosophy of Physics). Cambridge University Press.

Brivio, Ilaria, and Michael Trott. 2019. The standard model as an effective field theory. *Physics Reports*, 793:1–98.

Burgess, Cliff. 2021. *Introduction to Effective Field Theory: Thinking Effectively about Hierarchies of Scale* (1st ed.). Cambridge University Press.

Butterfield, Jeremy. 2011. Less is different: Emergence and reduction reconciled. *Foundations of Physics*, 41(6):1065–1135.

Butterfield, Jeremy. 2014. Reduction, emergence, and renormalization. *The Journal of Philosophy*, 111(1):5–49.

Butterfield, Jeremy, and Nazim Bouatta. 2015. Renormalization for philosophers. In Tomasz Bigaj and Christian Wüthrich (eds.). *Metaphysics in Contemporary Physics*, volume 104 of Poznan Studies in the Philosophy of the Sciences and the Humanities, pages 437–485. Brill.

Cardy, John. 1996. *Scaling and Renormalization in Statistical Physics*. Cambridge University Press.

Chakravartty, Anjan. 2007. *A Metaphysics for Scientific Realism: Knowing the Unobservable*. Cambridge University Press.

Chen, Lu. 2022. Can we "effectivize" spacetime? *Studies in History and Philosophy of Science*: 75–83.

Clifton, Rob, and Hans Halvorson. 2001. Entanglement and open systems in algebraic quantum field theory. *Studies in History and Philosophy of Science Part B: Studies in History and Philosophy of Modern Physics*, 32(1): 1–31.

Cohen, Timothy. 2020. As scales become separated: Lectures on effective field theory. *arXiv preprint: 1903.03622.*

Coleman, Sidney. 1985. *Aspects of Symmetry: Selected Erice Lectures*. Cambridge University Press.

Coleman, Sidney. 2019. *Quantum Field Theory: Lectures of Sidney Coleman*. World Scientific.

Collins, John C. 1984. *Renormalization: An Introduction to Renormalization, the Renormalization Group, and the Operator-Product Expansion*. Cambridge University Press.

Contino, Roberto, Adam Falkowski, Florian Goertz, Christophe Grojean, and Francesco Riva. 2016. On the validity of the effective field theory approach to SM precision tests. *Journal of High Energy Physics*, 2016(7): 1–26.

Crispino, Luis CB, Atsushi Higuchi, and George EA Matsas. 2008. The Unruh effect and its applications. *Reviews of Modern Physics*, 80(3):787–838.

Davidson, Sacha, Paolo Gambino, Mikko Laine, Matthias Neubert, and Christophe Salomon. 2020. *Effective Field Theory in Particle Physics and Cosmology: Lecture Notes of the Les Houches Summer School: Volume 108, July 2017*. Oxford University Press.

de Rham, Claudia, Sandipan Kundu, Matthew Reece, Andrew J Tolley, and Shuang-Yong Zhou. 2022. Snowmass white paper: UV constraints on IR physics. *arXiv preprint: 2203.06805*.

Delamotte, Bertrand. 2012. An introduction to the nonperturbative renormalization group. In Achim Schwenk, Janos Polonyi (eds.). *Renormalization Group and Effective Field Theory Approaches to Many-Body Systems*, pages 49–132. Springer.

Dirac, Paul AM. 1933/2005. The Lagrangian in quantum mechanics. In Laurie M Brown, ed., *Feynman's Thesis: A New Approach to Quantum Theory*, pages 111–119. World Scientific.

Duncan, Anthony. 2012. *The Conceptual Framework of Quantum Field Theory*. Oxford University Press.

Earman, John. 2011. The Unruh effect for philosophers. *Studies in History and Philosophy of Science Part B: Studies in History and Philosophy of Modern Physics*, 42(2):81–97.

Earman, John, and Doreen Fraser. 2006. Haag's theorem and its implications for the foundations of quantum field theory. *Erkenntnis*, 64(3):305–344.

Ellis, John, Christopher W Murphy, Verónica Sanz, and Tevong You. 2018. Updated global SMEFT fit to Higgs, diboson and electroweak data. *Journal of High Energy Physics*, 2018(6):1–34.

Esfeld, Michael. 2009. The modal nature of structures in ontic structural realism. *International Studies in the Philosophy of Science*, 23(2):179–194.

Feynman, Richard. 1948. Space-time approach to non-relativistic quantum mechanics. *Reviews of Modern Physics*, 20(2):367–387.

Forgione, Marco. 2020. Path integrals and holism. *Foundations of Physics*, 50 (8):799–827.

Franklin-Hall, Laura. 2016. High-level explanation and the interventionist's "variables problem." *The British Journal for the Philosophy of Science*, 67(2):553–577.

Fraser, Doreen. 2008. The fate of "particles" in quantum field theories with interactions. *Studies in History and Philosophy of Science Part B: Studies in History and Philosophy of Modern Physics*, 39(4):841–859.

Fraser, Doreen. 2009. Quantum field theory: Underdetermination, inconsistency, and idealization. *Philosophy of Science*, 76(4):536–567.

Fraser, Doreen. 2011. How to take particle physics seriously: A further defence of axiomatic quantum field theory. *Studies in History and Philosophy of Science Part B: Studies in History and Philosophy of Modern Physics*, 42 (2):126–135.

Fraser, Doreen. 2021. Particles in quantum field theory. In Eleanor Knox and Alistair Wilson, eds., *The Routledge Companion to the Philosophy of Physics*, pages 232–336. Routledge.

Fraser, James D. 2018. Renormalization and the formulation of scientific realism. *Philosophy of Science*, 85(5):1164–1175.

Fraser, James D. 2020. Towards a realist view of quantum field theory. In Steven French and Juha Saatsi, eds., *Scientific Realism and the Quantum*, pages 276–291. Oxford University Press.

Georgi, Howard. 1993. Effective field theory. *Annual Review of Nuclear and Particle Science*, 43(1):209–252.

Giudice, Gian F. 2013. Naturalness after LHC8. *arXiv preprint: 1307.7879*.

Giudice, Gian Francesco. 2017. The dawn of the post-naturalness era. *arXiv preprint: 1710.07663*.

Haag, Rudolf. 1996. *Local Quantum Physics* (2nd ed.). Springer.

Halvorson, Hans. 2001. Reeh–Schlieder defeats Newton–Wigner: On alternative localization schemes in relativistic quantum field theory. *Philosophy of Science*, 68(1):111–133.

Halvorson, Hans, and Rob Clifton. 2002. No place for particles in relativistic quantum theories? *Philosophy of Science*, 69(1):1–28.

Henning, Brian, Xiaochuan Lu, and Hitoshi Murayama. 2016. How to use the standard model effective field theory. *Journal of High Energy Physics*, 2016(1):1–97.

Itzykson, Claude, and Jean-Bernard Zuber. 1980. *Quantum Field Theory*. McGraw-Hill.

Kaiser, David. 2009. *Drawing Theories Apart*. University of Chicago Press.

Kitcher, Philip. 1993. *The Advancement of Science: Science without Legend, Objectivity without Illusions*. Oxford University Press.

Kuhlmann, Meinard. 2010. Why conceptual rigour matters to philosophy: On the ontological significance of algebraic quantum field theory. *Foundations of Physics*, 40(9–10):1625–1637.

Ladyman, James, Don Ross, David Spurrett, and John Collier. 2007, *Every Thing Must Go: Metaphysics Naturalized*. Oxford University Press.

Laudan, Larry. 1981. A confutation of convergent realism. *Philosophy of Science*, 48:19–49.

Lee, Benjamin W, Ch Quigg, and HB Thacker. 1977a. Strength of weak interactions at very high energies and the Higgs boson mass. *Physical Review Letters*, 38(16):883–885.

Lee, Benjamin W, Chris Quigg, and HB Thacker. 1977b. Weak interactions at very high energies: The role of the Higgs-boson mass. *Physical Review D*, 16(5):1519–1531.

Malament, David. 1996. In defense of dogma: Why there cannot be a relativistic quantum mechanics of (localizable) particles. In Rob Clifton, ed., *Perspectives on Quantum Reality*, pages 1–10. Springer.

Manohar, Aneesh. 2020. Introduction to effective field theories. In Sacha Davidson, Paolo Gambino, Mikko Laine, Matthias Neubert, and Christophe Salomon, eds., *Effective Field Theory in Particle Physics and Cosmology: Lecture Notes of the Les Houches Summer School: Volume 108, July 2017*. pages 47–136. Oxford University Press.

Miller, Michael E. 2018. Haag's theorem, apparent inconsistency, and the empirical adequacy of quantum field theory. *The British Journal for the Philosophy of Science*, 69(3):801–820.

Mukhanov, Viatcheslav, and Sergei Winitzki. 2007. *Introduction to Quantum Effects in Gravity*. Cambridge University Press.

Penco, Riccardo. 2020. An introduction to effective field theories. *arXiv preprint: 2006.16285*.

Peskin, Michael, and Daniel Schroeder. 1995. *An Introduction to Quantum Field Theory*. Westview Press.

Petrov, Alexey A, and Andrew E Blechman. 2016. *Effective Field Theories*. World Scientific.

Polchinski, Joseph. 1984. Renormalization and effective lagrangians. *Nuclear Physics B*, 231(2):269–295.

Psillos, Stathis. 1999. *Scientific Realism: How Science Tracks Truth*. Routledge.

Redhead, Michael. 1995. More ado about nothing. *Foundations of Physics*, 25 (1):123–137.

Remmen, Grant N, and Nicholas L Rodd. 2019. Consistency of the standard model effective field theory. *Journal of High Energy Physics*, 2019(12): 1–52.

Rivat, Sébastien. 2019. Renormalization scrutinized. *Studies in History and Philosophy of Science Part B: Studies in History and Philosophy of Modern Physics*, 68:23–39.

Rivat, Sébastien, and Alexei Grinbaum. 2020. Philosophical foundations of effective field theories. *The European Physical Journal A*, 56(3):1–10.

Roberts, Bryan W. 2011. Group structural realism. *The British Journal for the Philosophy of Science*, 62(1):47–69.

Rosaler, Joshua, and Robert Harlander. 2019. Naturalness, Wilsonian renormalization, and "fundamental parameters" in quantum field theory. *Studies in History and Philosophy of Science Part B: Studies in History and Philosophy of Modern Physics*, 66:118–134.

Ruetsche, Laura. 2011. *Interpreting Quantum Theories*. Oxford University Press.

Ruetsche, Laura. 2018. Renormalization group realism: The ascent of pessimism. *Philosophy of Science*, 85(5):1176–1189.

Ruetsche, Laura. 2020. Perturbing realism. In Steven French and Juha Saatsi, eds., *Scientific Realism and the Quantum*, pages 293–314. Oxford University Press.

Ryder, Lewis H. 1996. *Quantum Field Theory*. Cambridge University Press.

Saatsi, Juha. 2022. (In)effective realism. *European Journal of Philosophy of Science*, 12:1–16.

Sachdev, Subir. 2011. *Quantum Phase Transitions*. Cambridge University Press.

Schwartz, Matthew D. 2014. *Quantum Field Theory and the Standard Model*. Cambridge University Press.

Schweber, Silvan S. 1994. *QED and the Men Who Made It: Dyson, Feynman, Schwinger, and Tomonaga*. Princeton University Press.

Sebens, Charles. 2022. The fundamentality of fields. *Synthese*, 200, 380.

Shifman, Mikhail. 2012. *Advanced Topics in Quantum Field Theory*. Cambridge University Press.

Srednicki, Mark. 2007. *Quantum Field Theory*. Cambridge University Press.

Streater, Ray F, and Arthur S Wightman. 1964. *PCT, Spin and Statistics, and All That*. W. A. Benjamin.

Strocchi, Franco. 2013. *An Introduction to Non-Perturbative Foundations of Quantum Field Theory*. Oxford University Press.

Swanson, Noel. 2017. A philosopher's guide to the foundations of quantum field theory. *Philosophy Compass*, 12(5): e12414.

Swanson, Noel. forthcoming. *Philosophy of Quantum Field Theory* (Elements in the Philosophy of Physics). Cambridge University Press.

Tan, Peter. 2019. Counterpossible non-vacuity in scientific practice. *The Journal of Philosophy*, 116(1):32–60.

van Fraassen, Bas. 1980. *The Scientific Image*. Oxford University Press.

Wald, Robert M. 1994. *Quantum Field Theory in Curved Spacetime and Black Hole Thermodynamics*. University of Chicago Press.

Weinberg, Steven. 1977. The search for unity: Notes for a history of quantum field theory. *Daedalus: Volume 06*, 17–35.

Weinberg, Steven. 1983. Why the renormalization group is a good thing. In Alan Guth, Kerson Huang, and Robert L Jaffe, eds., *Asymptotic Realms of Physics: Essays in Honor of Francis Low*, pages 1–19. The MIT Press.

Weinberg, Steven. 1995. *The Quantum Theory of Fields*, volume 1: Foundations. Cambridge University Press.

Wells, James D. 2015. The utility of naturalness, and how its application to quantum electrodynamics envisages the standard model and Higgs boson. *Studies in History and Philosophy of Science Part B: Studies in History and Philosophy of Modern Physics*, 49:102–108.

Williams, Porter. 2015. Naturalness, the autonomy of scales, and the 125 GeV Higgs. *Studies in History and Philosophy of Science Part B: Studies in History and Philosophy of Modern Physics*, 51:82–96.

Williams, Porter. 2017. Scientific realism made effective. *The British Journal for the Philosophy of Science*, 70: 209–237.

Williams, Porter. 2019. Two notions of naturalness. *Foundations of Physics*, 49 (9):1022–1050.

Wilson, Alastair. 2021. Counterpossible reasoning in physics. *Philosophy of Science*, 88(5):1113–1124.

Wilson, Kenneth G, and John Kogut. 1974. The renormalization group and the ε expansion. *Physics Reports*, 12(2):75–199.

Wimsatt, William C. 2007. *Re-Engineering Philosophy for Limited Beings: Piecewise Approximations to Reality*. Harvard University Press.

Witten, Edward. 2001. Quantum gravity in de Sitter space. *arXiv preprint: hep-th/0106109*.

Witten, Edward. 2018. APS medal for exceptional achievement in research: Invited article on entanglement properties of quantum field theory. *Reviews of Modern Physics*, 90(4):045003.

Woodward, James. 2021a. *Causation with a Human Face*. Oxford University Press.

Woodward, James. 2021b. Explanatory autonomy: The role of proportionality, stability, and conditional irrelevance. *Synthese*, 198(1):237–265.

Worrall, John. 1989. Structural realism: The best of both worlds? *Dialectica*, 43:99–124.

Yablo, Stephen. 1992. Mental causation. *The Philosophical Review*, 101(2): 245–280.

Zee, Anthony. 2010. *Quantum Field Theory in a Nutshell* (2nd ed.). Princeton University Press.

Cambridge Elements ≡

The Philosophy of Physics

James Owen Weatherall

University of California, Irvine

James Owen Weatherall is Professor of Logic and Philosophy of Science at the University of California, Irvine. He is the author, with Cailin O'Connor, of *The Misinformation Age: How False Beliefs Spread* (Yale, 2019), which was selected as a *New York Times* Editors' Choice and Recommended Reading by *Scientific American*. His previous books were *Void: The Strange Physics of Nothing* (Yale, 2016) and the *New York Times* bestseller *The Physics of Wall Street: A Brief History of Predicting the Unpredictable* (Houghton Mifflin Harcourt, 2013). He has published approximately fifty peer-reviewed research articles in journals in leading physics and philosophy of science journals and has delivered over 100 invited academic talks and public lectures.

About the Series

This Cambridge Elements series provides concise and structured introductions to all the central topics in the philosophy of physics. The Elements in the series are written by distinguished senior scholars and bright junior scholars with relevant expertise, producing balanced, comprehensive coverage of multiple perspectives in the philosophy of physics.

Cambridge Elements =

The Philosophy of Physics